ROUTLEDGE LIBRARY EDITIONS:
SOVIET POLITICS

I0124478

Volume 23

THE SOVIET UNION

THE SOVIET UNION

Second Edition

Edited by
R. W. DAVIES
AND
DENIS J. B. SHAW

Routledge
Taylor & Francis Group

LONDON AND NEW YORK

First published in 1989 by Unwin Hyman

This edition first published in 2024
by Routledge
4 Park Square, Milton Park, Abingdon, Oxon OX14 4RN

and by Routledge
605 Third Avenue, New York, NY 10158

Routledge is an imprint of the Taylor & Francis Group, an informa business

British Library Cataloguing in Publication Data
A catalogue record for this book is available from the British Library

ISBN: 978-1-032-67165-9 (Set)
ISBN: 978-1-032-67633-3 (Volume 23) (hbk)
ISBN: 978-1-032-67635-7 (Volume 23) (pbk)
ISBN: 978-1-032-67634-0 (Volume 23) (ebk)

DOI: 10.4324/9781032676340

Publisher's Note
The publisher has gone to great lengths to ensure the quality of this reprint but points out that some imperfections in the original copies may be apparent.

Disclaimer
The publisher has made every effort to trace copyright holders and would welcome correspondence from those they have been unable to trace.

THE
SOVIET UNION

Second Edition

———

Edited by

R. W. Davies

Professor of Soviet Economic Studies
Centre for Russian and East European Studies
University of Birmingham

with the assistance of

Denis J. B. Shaw

Department of Geography
University of Birmingham

Boston
UNWIN HYMAN
London   Sydney   Wellington

Unwin Hyman, Inc.
8 Winchester Place, Winchester, Mass. 01890, USA

Published by the Academic Division of
Unwin Hyman Ltd
15/17 Broadwick Street, London W1V 1FP, UK

Allen & Unwin (Australia) Ltd,
8 Napier Street, North Sydney, NSW 2060, Australia

Allen & Unwin (New Zealand) Ltd in association with the
Port Nicholson Press Ltd,
60 Cambridge Terrace, Wellington, New Zealand

First Edition published in 1978.
Second Edition published in 1989.

Library of Congress Cataloging in Publication Data

The Soviet Union / edited by R. W. Davies; with the assistance of
Denis J. B. Shaw. — 2nd ed.
  p.   cm.
Bibliography: p.
Includes index.
ISBN 0–04–445205–5.   ISBN 0–04–445215–2 (pbk.)
1. Soviet Union — Civilization — 1917–   I. Davies, R. W. (Robert
William), 1925–   .   II. Shaw, Denis J. B.
DK266.4.S68   1988   88–19010
947'. 08 — dc 19   CIP

British Library Cataloguing in Publication Data

The Soviet Union. — 2nd ed.
  1. Soviet Union, 1917–
  I. Davies, R. W. (Robert William),
  II. Shaw, Denis J. B.
  947.084
  ISBN 0–04–445205–5
      0–04–445215–2 pbk

Typeset in 10 on 12pt Bembo by Nene Phototypesetters Ltd, Northampton
and printed in Great Britain by Billing and Son Ltd, London and Worcester

Contents

Acknowledgements

Figure 4   Office of Population Research, Princeton University

Figures 6 & 7   G. D. H. Cole's estate and Penguin Books Ltd.

Figure 8   The late Professor Leonard Schapiro

Figure 9   The Copyright Agency of the USSR and the editors of *EKO*

Figure 10   University of Birmingham

Figures 16 & 17   Mr Martin Gilbert (drawn with amendments from his *Russian History Atlas*, Weidenfeld & Nicholson, London, 1970)

Preface

The Soviet Union provides a general introduction to the contemporary Soviet Union for sixth-formers and non-specialist students. It was originally based on a short course provided annually for first-year students at Birmingham University, whose main fields of study range from engineering to fine arts.

The importance of the subject is beyond doubt. The Soviet Union is by far the largest country in the world, occupying as much as one-sixth of the earth's surface, and is perhaps better endowed with mineral wealth than any other country. It is second only to the United States in total industrial production and, together with the United States, is one of the two military superpowers.

But the significance of the Soviet Union in the modern world extends far beyond its economic and military might. Ever since the Revolution of October 1917, it has offered the challenge of what claims to be a new social, economic and political order – a planned socialist system. Together with the other countries that form the Communist world, the Soviet Union (officially known as the Union of Soviet Socialist Republics) presents an alternative to Western capitalism in both ideology and organisation.

No consensus exists about the nature of the Soviet alternative or the extent of its success. Marxist is divided from Marxist, non-Marxist from non-Marxist. Some Marxists see Soviet developments as a successful adaptation of Marx's doctrines to the conditions of a developing country; for them, the Soviet Union today is a genuinely socialist state, carrying the torch for the rest of the world. For other Marxists, such an assessment is a distortion and a betrayal of Marxism: the Soviet Union is a new kind of class society, dominated by a privileged bureaucracy, and no element of socialism remains. Non-Marxists also differ strongly among themselves. Some argue that much that is positive can be learned from Soviet experience. They believe that poor countries like India, while avoiding Soviet mistakes, can base themselves on Soviet planned industrialisation to bring speedy economic progress to their hungry masses. But other non-Marxists reject the Soviet system as undemocratic, bureaucratic, illiberal, and inhumane; according to them, it should be studied as a foremost example of what not to do.

For an understanding of modern Soviet society it is, therefore, particularly important to be aware not only of the agreed facts but also of the principal issues involved in assessing them. The 13 authors of the present volume, all specialists on the themes of their own chapters, have endeavoured both to provide the basic facts about their subjects and to introduce the readers to major disputes and unsolved problems. The book has been deliberately constructed to provoke informed controversy; it will soon become clear to the reader that the individual authors differ considerably among themselves in their approaches to the study of the Soviet Union.

The first edition of this volume was published in 1978 as *The Soviet Union*. Six of the 14 chapters in the present volume are entirely new, and the remaining chapters have been revised.

Great changes are taking place in the Soviet Union; international and internal events are moving rapidly, and a serious effort is being made to carry through major reforms of the system. This upheaval has been in the forefront of our minds in writing or revising our chapters. We have not refrained from trying to peer ahead into the Soviet future, albeit with due academic caution.

It is also important to see present developments in historical perspective. The Soviet system was established in a specific country at a specific time, and we are firmly convinced that it is impossible to make a satisfactory assessment of the system without some knowledge of the historical background and culture of the Russians and other peoples who make up the Soviet Union, and of the international context in which the Soviet Revolution took place and was consolidated. Therefore, we begin our account with a consideration of the geography and history of the Soviet Union (Chs 1–4) before turning to the present political, social and economic system, and the efforts to adapt it to the requirements of the closing years of the twentieth century (Chs 5–9). We then discuss two important aspects of Soviet life and culture: education and the arts (Chs 10 and 11). Further chapters place Soviet developments in their past and present international context (Chs 12 and 13). The brief concluding chapter draws attention to the major controversies referred to in the course of the book and to the divergent opinions expressed by different authors (it also presents my own opinion). A list of major dates and a glossary are designed to help the reader who is unfamiliar with the Soviet scene. A bibliography, divided by subjects, provides a guide to further reading.

Dr Denis J. B. Shaw was responsible for collecting the photographs and preparing maps and diagrams; I am most grateful to him for his efficient help.

The authors also wish to express their thanks to Tim Grogan, who drew or redrafted the maps and diagrams, to Pat Short, who drew the illustrations from the first edition, and to Ms Irene Brezowski, photo librarian at the Society for Cultural Relations with the USSR, for her most efficient and willing help with the photographs. They also wish to thank Lisa Freeman and Michael Holdsworth, present and past editors at Unwin Hyman, for their helpful advice and encouragement, and Betty Bennett, Nancy Moore and Anthea Roth for efficiently preparing the typescript for the publisher.

R. W. Davies
University of Birmingham

Notes on the Contributors

R. W. Davies is Professor of Soviet Economic Studies at the Centre for Russian and East European Studies of the University of Birmingham and was Director of the Centre from 1963–78. He is the author of *The Development of the Soviet Budgetary System, Foundations of a Planned Economy 1926–1929*, vol. 1 (with E. H. Carr), and a multi-volume history of Soviet industrialisation. The third volume of this history, *The Soviet Economy in Turmoil, 1929–1930*, has just been published.

Denis J. B. Shaw is Lecturer in Soviet Geography in the Department of Geography and Associate member of the Centre for Russian and East European Studies, University of Birmingham. He is a specialist on the settlement of early Russia and has published many articles on Soviet urban and regional planning. He is a co-author of *Planning of the Soviet Union* and *Landscape and Settlement in Romanov Russia*.

Maureen Perrie is Lecturer in the Centre for Russian and East European Studies and the School of History, University of Birmingham. She is the author of *The Agrarian Policy of the Russian Socialist Revolutionary Party from its Origins through the Revolution of 1905–7* and *The Image of Ivan the Terrible in Russian Folk-Lore*.

M. Lewin is Professor of History at the University of Pennsylvania in Philadelphia and was previously Professor of Soviet History and Politics in the Centre for Russian and East European Studies, University of Birmingham. He is the author of *Russian Peasants and Soviet Power, Lenin's Last Struggle, Political Undercurrents in Soviet Economic Debates*, and *The Making of the Soviet System*.

Ronald Amann is Director of the Centre for Russian and East European Studies and Professor of Soviet Politics, University of Birmingham. He specialises in science policy and the interplay between economic and political change in the USSR. Recently, with Julian Cooper, he edited an inter-university study on *Technical Progress and Soviet Economic Development*.

David Lane is Professor of Sociology in the Centre for Russian and East European Studies, University of Birmingham, and a former Fellow of

Emmanuel College, Cambridge. He is the author of *State and Politics in the USSR, Soviet Economy and Society, Soviet Labour and the Ethic of Communism*, and several other studies on politics and society in the Soviet Union and Eastern Europe.

Philip Hanson is a Professor of Soviet Economics at the University of Birmingham. His research has been mainly on the Soviet domestic economy and on East–West trade. His books include *Trade and Technology in Soviet–Western Relations*. His articles on the Soviet economy have appeared in *Radio Liberty Research, Soviet Studies*, and *Soviet Economy*, and he has also written for *The Times, Wall Street Journal*, and *The Guardian*.

Julian Cooper is Lecturer in Soviet Technology and Industry, Centre for Russian and East European Studies, University of Birmingham. Publications include *The Technological Level of Soviet Industry*, edited with Ronald Amann and R. W. Davies, *Industrial Innovation in the Soviet Union*, edited jointly with Ronald Amann, and articles on Soviet industry, science and technology, and economic history. He is Editor of the journal *Economics of Planning*.

R. E. F. Smith was formerly Head of the Department of Russian Language and Literature, University of Birmingham, and is the author of several books on farming in Russia from early times, including *The Enserfment of the Russian Peasantry, Peasant Farming in Muscovy*, and (with David Christian) *Bread and Salt*. He is also compiler of the *Russian–English Dictionary of Social Science Terms*, a new edition of which is in preparation.

John Dunstan is Senior Lecturer in the Centre for Russian and East European Studies and the Faculty of Education, University of Birmingham, and Deputy Director of the Centre. He is the author of *Paths to Excellence and the Soviet School* as well as many articles on Soviet education, and editor of *Soviet Education under Scrutiny*.

G. S. Smith is Professor of Russian in the University of Oxford and Fellow of New College. He has taught at the universities of Nottingham, Birmingham, Liverpool, Indiana, and California at Berkeley. He is a specialist on 18th-century Russian literature and also writes on recent Russian poetry; he is the author of *Songs to Seven Strings: Russian Guitar Poetry and Soviet 'Mass Song'*.

Jonathan G. Haslam is Senior Research Fellow in Politics at King's College, Cambridge University. From 1975 to 1984, he was Lecturer in Soviet Diplomatic History at the University of Birmingham; from 1984 to

1988, he taught at various universities in the United States. He is the author of *Soviet Foreign Policy, 1930–33: The Impact of the Depression* and *The Soviet Union and the Struggle for Collective Security in Europe, 1933–39.*

David Holloway is Professor of Political Science and Member of the Center for International Security and Arms Control at Stanford University. He is the author of *The Soviet Union and the Arms Race* and a co-author of *The Reagan Strategic Defense Initiative: A Technical, Political and Arms Control Assessment.* He contributed to Amann, Cooper, and Davies (eds.) *The Technological Level of Soviet Industry* and to Amann and Cooper (eds.) *Industrial Innovation in the Soviet Union.*

1

The Geographical Reality

DENIS J. B. SHAW

Physical environment, with its many dimensions, provides people and their organisations with both opportunities and limitations. Even a modern and highly organised state, such as the Union of Soviet Socialist Republics (USSR), cannot overlook the facts of geography, sometimes blatant but more often subtly felt, that inexorably bring their influence to bear upon human activity. This chapter investigates some of the most obvious of these influences and traces their consequences.

SIZE AND ITS CONSEQUENCES

The USSR is by far the largest nation in the world. Covering an area of 22.4 million square kilometres (8.6 million square miles), it is more than twice the size of China or the United States and no less than ninety times the size of the United Kingdom, amounting to 15 per cent of the entire land surface of the world. From west to east, the USSR stretches through 10 000 kilometres, or eleven time zones. For those who normally visualise the United States and the Soviet Union as occupying opposite sides of the northern hemisphere, it is salutary to remember that the westernmost tip of the United States in Alaska (Prince of Wales Cape) is only 90 kilometres from Cape Dezhnev, the easternmost point of Siberia. The two are separated by the grey waters of the Bering Strait, which freezes over in winter.

From north to south, the longest axis across the USSR is somewhat less (4800 kilometres), but along this axis the physical changes are very great. The northernmost point of Soviet territory, on the islands of Franz Josef Land, experiences subzero temperatures throughout virtually the entire year and is situated only a few

1

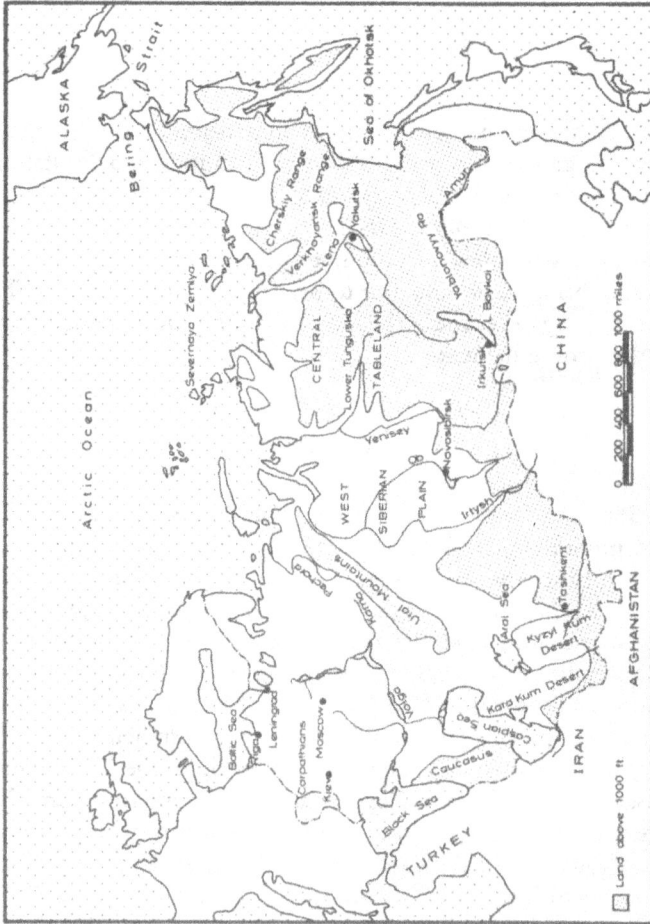

Figure 1 *The USSR: major physical features and cities*

hundred kilometres from the North Pole. The southernmost portion of Soviet territory lies on the borders of Afghanistan and within a short distance of the frontiers of India and Pakistan (Fig. 1). The USSR is truly a giant among nations.

Vastness brings both advantages and disadvantages to a nation. Territory must be held and administered, involving costly communications over long distances. In the past, communications could be exceedingly slow. The Russians attempted to make maximum use of their long and slow-flowing rivers for transportation (though the northward-flowing Siberian rivers were of limited use in this respect) and in winter had recourse to the sledge; but many outlying provinces remained extremely remote from the centre of power in the days of the Tsarist Empire. An old Russian proverb, 'God is in his heaven, and the Tsar far away', reflects the isolation of the provincial governor of those days, and there can be little wonder that many governors ruled their districts like personal fiefs. Communications even today are often difficult and expensive. The average length of haul for goods travelling by rail is considerable, and many northern and eastern settlements, remote from the main centres of population and the networks of road and rail, can be reached only by air or water.

Travel by air is very popular in the Soviet Union especially in less populated regions. (*Society for Cultural Relations with the USSR, London*)

3

Defence of such a vast territory is complicated and difficult. The Soviet Union shares land borders with 12 other countries, and her seacoast, including the many offshore islands, is exceedingly long. High mountains to the south and east, however, have rendered defence somewhat easier; in past centuries, the only really major challenge to Russia in this area (apart from the British in India) came from the Chinese, who in the 17th century successfully checked the eastward Russian advance. For a time at the beginning of the present century, Japan menaced Russia from the east; in the past 35 years, a reinvigorated China has again asserted herself and in Soviet eyes sometimes seems to threaten both Central Asia and the Far East.

To the west, by contrast, the Soviet frontiers have little natural protection. Russian and Soviet history has been characterised by a series of major invasions from the west — by the Poles in the 17th century, the Swedes in the 18th century, Napoleon and his Grand Army in 1812, and twice by the Germans in the present century. During the German invasion of 1941–45, more than 20 million Soviet lives were lost, with a devastating effect on the Soviet labour force. This momentous fact, coupled with the need to protect the many outlying and vulnerable areas, helps explain the heavy Soviet emphasis on defence, with a huge defence budget, a large programme of national service, and much military propaganda.

On the other hand, the vast territory of the USSR has been an important strategic resource as well as a liability. This was amply demonstrated by the defence-in-depth strategy successfully used by the Russians both in 1812 and from 1941 to 1945.

Over this huge Soviet territory natural conditions vary enormously. This is important from the point of view of both natural resources and land use. About half the territory of the USSR, for example, lies within the boreal forest zone, dominated by the northern coniferous forests. This zone makes the Soviet Union the world's most important possessor of softwoods (Fig. 2). Much of this softwood, especially in the east, is poorly exploited, but in the more populated regions to the west the heavy demand for timber for paper, construction, and wood chemicals leads to overcutting in many areas. To the south of the boreal forest and the zone of mixed forest, lie the forest-steppe and steppe grasslands, which are coincidental with the rich *chernozem* or black-earth soils. The black earths are among the world's most fertile soils, and consequently the steppe grasslands are now almost entirely ploughed for grain. Other

Figure 2   *The USSR: major natural regions*

resources of this type include the huge rivers, which make a substantial contribution to the power industry through the highly developed network of hydroelectric power stations, and the extensive areas of peat bog, especially in the swampy areas in the north and west of European Russia, which even today supply a certain amount of peat fuel for power generation. Even climate is a resource. The USSR is large enough to include both the far north, where no cultivation of any type is possible, and such areas as Central Asia and the Transcaucasus, where subtropical products can be cultivated, including tea in the wetter parts of the Transcaucasus and cotton under irrigation in some drier locales.

Soviet natural resources include vast mineral wealth, and the Soviet Union is able to satisfy most mineral requirements from her own resources. But many minerals are poorly located relative to the Soviet population and the major industrial regions. Remote territories in the north, on the Central Siberian Plateau, and in the mountains of the Far East are exploited for gold, lead, zinc, diamonds, nickel, tin, copper, and apatite.

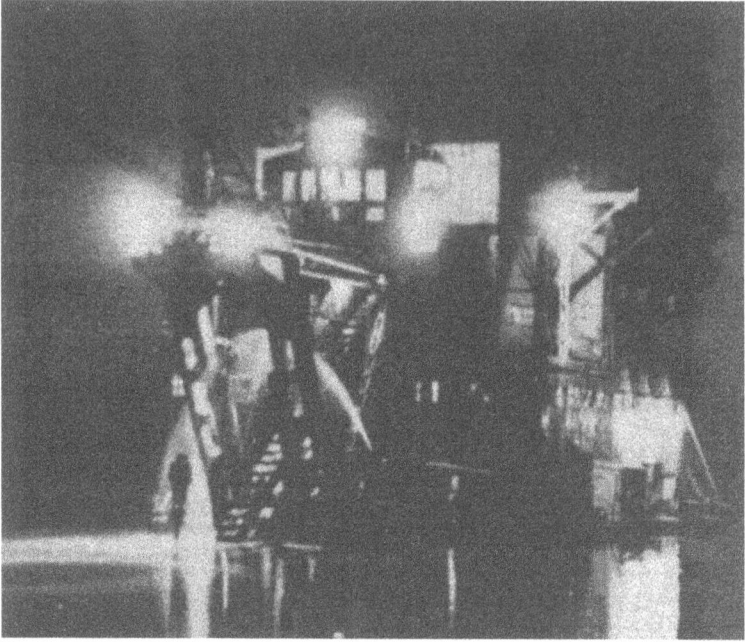

A diamond-extracting dredge on the remote Irelyakh River in the Yakutian taiga, north-eastern Siberia. (*SCR*)

Perhaps the most important of all Soviet natural resources are the sources of energy. Coal, oil, and natural gas account for more than 90 per cent of the fuel consumption of the Soviet Union, but she is having to turn to even remoter areas to satisfy energy needs. For coal, greater reliance is being placed on the eastern fields, such as the Kuzbass in West Siberia, because of the growing costs of mining in the Donbass in the south of the European USSR. Soviet coal reserves are huge (perhaps enough to last for several thousand years at present rates of extraction); but some of the biggest potential reserves lie in such hostile and inaccessible regions that they are unlikely to be exploited in the near future. The Soviet reserves of oil and natural gas are also extensive and make a major contribution to exports as well as to internal fuel supply. In recent years, West Siberia has become by far the most important region for the production of oil and natural gas in the USSR, accounting for almost two-thirds of oil production and almost 60 per cent of gas production by the mid-1980s. This is a remarkable achievement: oil deposits are mainly found under a vast swampland in the middle of the hostile West Siberian Plain, and the gas is found far to the north in the treeless tundra regions bordering the Arctic Ocean. Summer fog and savage winter wind are only two of the hazards threatening those who live and work in this bleak coastal environment.

All these examples illustrate not only the vast natural resources of the USSR but also major geographical and historical difficulties. Whereas many of the most important and promising Soviet natural resources, especially mineral resources, are to be found in the remoter north and east, the bulk of the population lives in the west and south — in European Russia and Central Asia. This discrepancy, discussed later in this chapter, poses enormous problems for communications, investment, and industrial development. Its solution is one of the most urgent tasks facing the Soviet economy today.

TERRITORIAL EXPANSION

The present vast size of the USSR is the product of a long period of evolution. The early history of the Russians and their kinsmen, the Ukrainians and Belorussians (together known as the Eastern Slavs), is lost in the mists of antiquity. In early medieval times, the Russians achieved a degree of political unity under the highly developed Kievan State, but this later fell apart due partly to internal squabbling. The Russian peoples particularly suffered under the depredations of the Mongols in the 13th century, and thereafter Russia was split into a series of loosely connected princedoms. One of these, the princedom of Moscow, gradually assumed pre-eminence and from the 14th century began to gather the others under its rule. By the middle of the 16th century, a united Muscovy was strong enough to challenge the successors to the Mongols (the Tatars) and began to expand both southward toward the Black Sea and eastward into Siberia. Referring to this process, the eminent Russian historian, V. O. Klyuchevskii, declared colonisation to be the dominating theme of Russian history. The first Russian settlement on the Pacific, Okhotsk, was established in 1647, and in 1696 the Russians took Azov, the key to the Black Sea. During the 17th and 18th centuries, a series of struggles against the Swedes, the Poles and the Turks expanded the Russian frontier westward to embrace the Gulf of Finland, the Baltic coast, the Ukraine, Poland

and the Crimea. In the 19th century, the Russians acquired Finland, subdued the peoples of the Caucasus and Central Asia, and annexed fresh territory in the Far East from China.

In the course of 600 years, Muscovy expanded many times over — from a mere few thousand square kilometres in the 14th century to more than 20 million by the time of the Bolshevik or Soviet Revolution of 1917. With some exceptions, notably Finland, Poland, and the Baltic states, all this territory came under the jurisdiction of the Soviet regime after 1917. The Baltic states were reannexed in 1940. The Soviet Union is thus almost coterminous with the pre-revolutionary Russian Empire. Although the new revolutionary government after 1917 at first denied the importance of territorial continuity with the Tsars, Soviet policies undoubtedly have been strongly influenced by this geographical and historical fact.

Territorial expansion on this scale means that the USSR today is not only a large state but also a multinational one. More than a hundred languages are spoken within her boundaries. The Russians are the linguistic and cultural majority, with 52 per cent of the total population; another 20 per cent are also Slavs. Other races include the Turkic and Iranian peoples of Central Asia, the Caucasians, the Baltic peoples, Finno-Ugrians, Mongols, and various minor groups. Almost all learn Russian, which is the major language for business and other purposes. The numerical preponderance of the Slavs is slowly diminishing, however, as birth rates among the Russians and other Slavs are significantly lower than among the peoples of Central Asia.

The administrative structure of the USSR caters to this racial diversity through its organisation as a federal state. The USSR consists of fifteen Union Republics, each of which corresponds to a major nationality. These Republics vary in size from the enormous Russian Federation, which occupies three-quarters of the entire country, to tiny Armenia. They have their own capitals, flags, official languages, and, theoretically, the right of secession. Lesser nationalities are often represented by Autonomous Soviet Socialist Republics (ASSRs) contained within the Union Republics. Finally, such entities as the Autonomous Oblast serve the national aspirations of minority groups. Each nationality is represented within the Soviet of Nationalities, one of the two houses of the Supreme Soviet (or parliament) in Moscow.

POSITION AND ITS CONSEQUENCES

Another factor of immense significance for the USSR is its position relative to the world's great oceans and continents. The country is situated astride the vast Eurasian landmass, the largest continuous land area in the world — what Sir Halford Mackinder, the eminent Oxford geographer, called 'the world island'. This means that much of the Soviet Union is situated far from the moderating influence of the world's oceans. Moreover, the Arctic Ocean, the one extensive body of water near Soviet territory, is frozen for most of the year. There can be little wonder, then, that most of the USSR suffers an extremely harsh continental climate, characterised by long, cold winters and rather short, hot summers.

The climatic consequences of this continental position are rendered more severe by two other factors. First, the absence of high mountains along the north coast means that the country is open to incursions of cold Arctic air, especially in winter, while mountains in the south cut off warm, moist air coming from the Indian Ocean. Late frosts and early autumns are frequent hazards for Soviet agriculture. Second, the northerly position of the Soviet Union adds to the severity and length of the winter. The historic core of the Russian nation, for example, lies fairly far to the north compared with the rest of Europe. Moscow lies roughly at the latitude of Edinburgh, Leningrad at that of the Shetland Islands. Approximately nine-tenths of the country is situated closer to the North Pole than to the equator.

Temperature and precipitation are the two great variables influencing the people and their activities in the USSR. The long, hard winter is usually characterised by anticyclonic conditions that discourage the formation of clouds and the incursion of moderating depressions. Stable air conditions and clear skies produce very low temperatures that actually worsen toward the east. Moscow, for example, experiences an average January temperature of about −10°C (14°F), whereas Novosibirsk in Siberia averages −19°C (−2°F). Within Siberia January temperatures drop especially quickly toward the northeast; around Verkhoyansk and Oymyakon, the world's 'cold pole', −50°C (−60°F) is common, and even lower temperatures have been recorded on occasions. Only the virtual absence of all air movement renders human life possible in such conditions.

9

A Siberian road in winter. (*SCR*)

Spring comes quickly in the USSR, and the melting snows and thawing rivers produce the period traditionally known as *rasputitsa* (the Thaw), a time of year notorious, especially in historic times, for floods and for appalling road conditions. Floods are especially prevalent at this time of year in Siberia, where the sources of the northward-flowing rivers naturally tend to thaw before the mouths far to the north.

Although the winter in the Soviet Union is noted for its low temperatures, the summer tends to be warm. In Moscow, July temperatures of 20°C (68°F) or more are common; in Central Asia, 30°C and even 40°C (85–105°F) are frequently experienced. On the Arctic coast, on the other hand, the temperature rarely rises much above freezing, and the Arctic islands remain frozen for almost the entire year.

The consequence of temperature variations in the USSR is that the temperature range between summer and winter, and hence the severity of the climate, increases toward the east. Thus, whereas the annual temperature range is around 24°C (43°F) in the Baltic states, Yakutia in northeastern Siberia has a range of up to 64°C (115°F). Both spring and autumn are shorter in Siberia than in the western part of the country.

The long winters and generally severe climate in the eastern and northern parts of the USSR render life especially difficult in these areas. The surrounding seas remain frozen for much of the year, and in the Arctic Ocean the reliable period for navigation is only about four months — even this is possible only through extensive use of icebreakers. Another problem is the permafrost (permanently frozen ground) that to a greater or lesser degree affects almost the whole of the northern and eastern parts of the USSR. Buildings constructed on permafrost need special and expensive protection against the danger of collapse. Other phenomena such as pingos, which are ice-cored hills domed up from beneath by the growth of ice, can disrupt roads, railways, and bridges.

The level of precipitation is as critical as temperature for human life and activity. Once again, the Soviet position on the Eurasian landmass has a decisive influence on the situation. Because the prevailing circulation pattern in the northern part of the northern hemisphere is west to east, the western part of the country receives more annual rainfall than do the central and eastern parts of Siberia. The prevailing pressure pattern, with conditions that are anticyclonic in winter and cyclonic in summer, ensures that most precipitation occurs during the summer period. However, the level of winter snow cover is particularly critical for agriculture. Here again the European part of the country is favoured, with a fairly thick cover over large areas. In contrast, the underlying soils in eastern Siberia, with its lower precipitation and thin, powdery snow cover, remain relatively unprotected against severe winter frosts.

The precipitation level falls even more sharply within the USSR as one travels southward. Within European Russia and the Ukraine, the forested lands give way in the south to the grasslands of the forest steppe and pure steppe (Fig. 2). Today most of this grassland is ploughed. East of the Urals, however, the steppe grasslands give way to semi-desert and finally to the pure deserts of Central Asia, with an average annual rainfall of less than 10 centimetres in many places. In these areas, population is largely restricted to the oases that bound the great rivers of the region.

11

Yalta, in the Crimea, has unusually mild winters by Soviet standards. (*SCR*)

There are two major exceptions to this overall climatic pattern. First, in extremely favoured regions on the southern extremity of the Crimean Peninsula and in parts of the western Transcaucasus, an unusually mild climate characterises the winter, and in keeping with the Mediterranean world in general, there tends to be a winter maximum of rainfall. These places are among the most popular in the USSR for holidaying purposes. Second, the Pacific coast of the Soviet Far East experiences a modified monsoon climate with a very heavy summer rainfall — one of the heaviest in the USSR.

From the point of view of human settlement, it is possible to divide the whole of the USSR into three major regions (Fig. 3). To the north and north-east, largely coinciding with the tundra and coniferous forest vegetation zones, is a vast territory in which the climate is too cold for successful agriculture, with the exception of some livestock farming, and where human settlement is consequently sparse. This is also a region where the temperatures are not high enough to evaporate the relatively low annual precipitation, and consequently there is an excess of moisture. This results in large areas of badly drained land and poor soils. Conditions are rendered

Figure 3   *The USSR: major settlement zones*

worse by the effects of the permafrost and the annual spring floods. Hence it is especially difficult to establish a large base of human settlement in this area, and the costs of exploiting the rich resources in minerals and timber are particularly high.

The second major region, which includes most of Central Asia, has high summer temperatures, and consequently high evaporation rates, but very low precipitation. This is an area of inadequate moisture, and the large desert lands can only be used during a very limited part of the year for grazing and not at all for cultivation. The latter is restricted to the oases where extensive irrigation networks exist, but where the dangers of salinisation and sand storms add to the difficulties of the situation.

The Soviet government has attempted various grandiose schemes to rectify the harsh climatic conditions of these two major regions. It is calculated that within the USSR as a whole a territory constituting 30 per cent of the country is characterised by only 2 per cent of the total surface water resources. To ameliorate these conditions, large new irrigation projects have been implemented, and under Stalin a

13

mammoth plan was inaugurated to extend the zone of adequate moisture southward by planting shelter belts of trees, with the aim of discouraging evaporation from the soil and even increasing rainfall. The Stalin plan was not a success. Even more ambitious were the various schemes to divert the northward-flowing rivers southward into water-deficient regions in Central Asia and around the Caspian. However, the costs and the considerable environmental complications of such schemes provoked serious controversy even after the plans were scaled down following Stalin's death. Official interest in river-diversion schemes revived in the 1970s, especially since the continual growth of population and industry worsened the water shortages in the south. But the diversion plans were cancelled by Gorbachev in 1986. Instead, emphasis will be placed on water conservation measures in the southern regions. It appears that the costs of the schemes, together with the pressures of conservationists, were the major factors behind this decision.

The Soviet government has also tried to improve conditions in the north by implementing large drainage and soil improvement schemes. Much experimentation has also been conducted to develop hardier crop species.

The third major region from the point of view of human settlement is the zone suitable for agriculture, including cultivation, where the bulk of the population lives. It coincides with the greater part of the European area and a relatively small zone parallel with the Trans-Siberian Railway in western and central Siberia. Here, and on the fringes of Central Asia, are situated the great majority of Soviet towns and industries. Even though this region is very large, it is small relative to the country as a whole. For example, 7.5 per cent of the total area of the USSR holds about half of its total population, whereas only 4.5 per cent of the total population inhabits 50 per cent of the total area. The arable area amounts to only about 10 per cent of the Soviet Union, and another 15 per cent can be used for grazing. The great discrepancy between the part of the USSR that has a majority of the population and the most favourable natural conditions and the part that has most of the natural wealth has already been alluded to as a major developmental problem.

Even within this region of maximum human settlement, however, conditions are often far from ideal. Reference has already been made to the hot summers and bitter winters, and even within this area the climate for agriculture is frequently difficult. It is estimated, for example, that only 15 per cent of farmland in the USSR has more than 170 frost-free days a year and that as much as 20 per cent is frost-free for 120 days or even fewer — a very short season indeed. As much as 40 per cent of the cropland receives 40 centimetres or less of rainfall a year, and very large areas are occasionally subject to drought. Agriculture in the USSR is notoriously unreliable in its productivity, and the fluctuations, undoubtedly worsened by low investment and other factors, are basically the product of a fickle climate.

Like all industrial countries, the Soviet Union suffers from the negative consequences of economic growth upon the natural environment: these include air and water pollution, waste disposal problems, and losses of land to building, flooding, and mineral exploitation. So far, the centrally planned economy has failed to deal adequately with such difficulties; some scholars argue that central- ised decision-making is an inappropriate mechanism for tackling what are often local issues. Nevertheless, since the 1950s the Soviet authorities have become more sensitive to environmental disrup- tion. They have developed a significant body of environmental legislation and have set up new organisations to monitor and control environmental policy. They have attempted to tie economic plann- ing more closely to environmental concerns and to use economic incentives to foster conservation. These measures have been only partially successful in protecting the environment, as the disaster at the Chernobyl nuclear power plant in April 1986 clearly demons- trated. It may be that the programme of economic reform (see Ch. 7) will lead to more far-reaching conservation policies. But the question remains whether economic growth can be reconciled with environmental protection in the long term. What is certain is that environmental disruption can only add to the problems faced by the Soviet people in attempting to build a modern economy in the context of an often unhelpful natural environment.

CONCLUSIONS: MAN AND NATURE IN THE USSR

The Soviet Union, then, is on the whole a difficult land in which to live. Nature there presents the inhabitants with manifold problems, although the opportunities, in terms of bountiful natural resources, are also great. Undoubtedly, one advantage that a belief in the

Birch trees, near Moscow, typical vegetation in the mixed forest region of central European Russia. (*SCR*)

principles of Marxism-Leninism, the official creed of the USSR, has brought to its people (or at least to its government) is an inherent optimism, a faith that people and their technology can win despite the enormous problems of nature that confront them. Unfortunately, in the past, and especially under Stalin, this faith in the power of science often led to hasty and unwise decisions, mammoth plans impossible to fulfil and a plundering and destructive attitude toward nature. Nowadays the Soviet authorities are more circumspect in these matters and more inclined to pay the natural environment the respect it deserves. Yet it is probably true to say that an underlying optimism still characterises the official view. Nature may be less pliable than was once believed, but as long as the Soviet authorities remain committed to further industrial development, they will continue to try to overcome the limitations nature imposes.

2

The October Revolution

MAUREEN PERRIE

PRE–REVOLUTIONARY RUSSIA

Chapter 1 shows how the vast territory of the Tsarist Empire, covering approximately the same area as the present–day USSR, had gradually been assembled by the end of the 19th century. At this time, Britain, France, Germany and the United States were already industrialised and modernised countries. But Tsarist Russia was an autocratic state with an overwhelmingly peasant population, which had been emancipated from serfdom only half a century before in 1861.

Russia was not, however, quite as backward as this general description would seem to imply. In the political field, the Tsar had been forced to permit the existence of a state Duma, or parliament, as a result of the revolutionary upheavals of 1905. This parliament was elected on the basis of an indirect and limited franchise, and its powers were severely restricted. Nevertheless, it did represent, together with the various elected local government bodies that had been created in 1864, some sort of basis for a more broadly democratic constitutional framework. There were many men of liberal views, both in the central Duma and in local government, who hoped and expected that the future political development of Russia lay in the extension of the powers of these existing institutions. A major obstacle to such an extension of democracy was the attitude of the Tsar himself. Nicholas II had a strong and almost mystical belief in his semi-divine role as autocrat, and in this belief he was strongly supported by his wife, the Empress Alexandra, who wanted the autocratic prerogatives of the Tsar to be passed on intact to their beloved son and heir, Alexei. Nicholas bitterly resented the concessions that had been wrung out of him by the

Tsar Nicholas II and his family in about 1905. (*Radio Times Hulton Picture Library*)

Revolution of 1905, and he was determined to yield nothing further to liberal opinion. Right-wing conservatives, including many of the landowning nobility, shared the Tsar's views.

In the economic field, the 19th century, particularly the decade of the 1890s, had seen a remarkable burst of industrialisation in Russia. This process continued, after a slight recession at the turn of the century, in the years preceding the outbreak of the First World War in 1914. Industrialisation resulted in the rapid growth of the major cities and in the formation of an industrial working class. But although the working class was growing several times faster than the population as a whole, on the eve of war it still represented only a tiny fraction of the total population (Fig. 4). Its potential political significance was nevertheless immense. It was concentrated in the major industrial cities, especially Moscow and the pre-Revolutionary capital of St. Petersburg, and was thus able to influence these centres of power in revolutionary situations, such as those of 1905 and 1917. Although the peasantry constituted the overwhelming majority of the population, they were scattered over the expanse of the Russian countryside in isolated villages and were therefore much more difficult to mobilise and organise for political purposes.

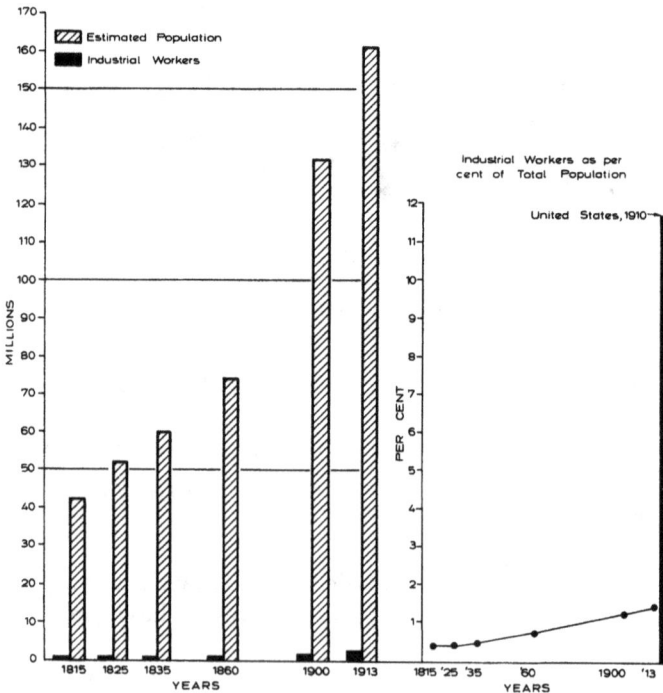

Figure 4 *Trend in number of industrial workers related to total population in the Russian Empire, 1815–1913*

'Now at last my people and I are at peace.' Cartoon of the 1905 Revolution and its aftermath. (*BPC Picture Library*)

In the years before 1914, therefore, there were many indications that Russia was, somewhat belatedly, setting out to follow the Western European path of development. Capitalist development in industry was accompanied by extensive reforms in peasant agriculture after 1905. The existence of the Duma not only provided representatives of the new business and professional classes with experience in government and administration but also served to

21

extend the political consciousness of the peasantry, familiarising them with the procedure of parliamentary elections. All this has led some historians to conclude that, had it not been for the intervention of the war, Russia would in all probability have followed a peaceful path of democratic capitalist development. The intransigence of the Tsar was a major obstacle, of course, but Nicholas could not live for ever.

If some historians take an optimistic view of the chances of peaceful development for Russia before the war, others argue that a violent overthrow of Tsarism was inevitable. They point to the deep divisions that still existed in Russian society and claim that the political and economic reforms that followed the 1905 Revolution had only scratched the surface of the problem. Millions of impoverished peasants coveted the large estates of the gentry. The urban workers had to endure appalling living and working conditions and very low wages. The educated classes were almost entirely alienated from the Tsarist government. In this unstable situation, all these discontents led in 1905 to widespread support for the underground revolutionary parties, and, according to these historians, revolutionary unrest was again widespread in the summer of 1914.

THE WAR AND THE FEBRUARY REVOLUTION

Immediately after the outbreak of the First World War, internal conflicts were thrust aside in a general upsurge of patriotic enthusiasm for the Tsar and the motherland. St. Petersburg, the German-sounding capital, was renamed Petrograd, and anti-German riots took place in Moscow. The wave of euphoria, however, did not last long. Russia was technologically backward, and the Tsarist government and the army general staff were incompetent and inefficient. The war was a major military disaster for Russia. Some responsibility for the defeats rested with the Imperial couple themselves. Against the advice of his ministers, Nicholas had personally assumed command of the army in 1915, leaving the everyday conduct of home affairs in the hands of the Empress. Alexandra was under the influence of an obscurantist group at court that was headed by Rasputin, the 'man of God' whose apparent powers to cure the bleeding of her only son, the haemophiliac Alexei, gave him a particular hold over the susceptible Empress.

By the third winter of the war, in 1916–17, public confidence in the Imperial government was at an all-time low, and the country was in the grip of a grave social and political crisis. The liberal opposition in the Duma openly accused the Tsar and the Empress of treason, and there was`a widespread feeling in society, and even in court circles, that the Tsar must go. The murder of Rasputin in December 1916 heralded plans for a palace *coup d'état*. But before these plans for bloodless reform from above could be implemented, they were forestalled by events from below. Food shortages in the capital were a major source of grievance, and in February 1917 widespread strikes, demonstrations and bread riots took place in Petrograd. They were followed by a mutiny of the troops called in to restore law and order. The government panicked; and with his capital in open revolt against him, the Tsar was forced to abdicate. A Provisional Government assumed power, consisting initially of the leaders of the liberal opposition in the Duma. At the same time, the revolutionary workers and soldiers, whose militant actions had caused the fall of the monarchy, formed their own councils, or Soviets. These Soviets assumed broad responsibilities for the day-to-day administration of the capital and the other major cities.

This simultaneous formation in February 1917 of the Provisional Government, on the one hand, and the Soviets, on the other, constituted the 'dual power' that led Lenin to decide that parliamentary government in Russia could and should be superseded by a government of the Soviets. Throughout the year, the Soviets and the Provisional Government fought a running battle over all the major issues. This conflict represented, in essence, a contest between those who had made the February Revolution — the militant workers and soldiers of Petrograd — and those who had benefited from it politically — the liberal members of the Provisional Government.

Throughout the summer of 1917, the Provisional Government lurched from one major ministerial crisis to another. The major bone of contention between the Government and the Soviets was the war with Germany. The liberal leaders of the Provisional Government had interpreted the events of February as a popular protest against the incompetent and inefficient conduct of the war, and they considered that the Revolution had given them, as the self-appointed leaders of Russian democracy, some kind of mandate to continue the war as a genuinely national effort. They felt that any far-reaching social reforms, such as a redistribution of the land (the age-old dream

23

Alexander Kerensky in exile. Kerensky was leader of the Provisional Government from July 1917. (*R T Hulton*)

of the Russian peasants), should be postponed, preferably until the war was won, but at least until such time as a general election could be held. A truly representative Constituent Assembly could then meet and implement reform measures that would enjoy democratically expressed popular support.

This policy of the Provisional Government, however, was based on a fatal misunderstanding of both the nature of the February Revolution and the mood of the people in 1917. The workers and soldiers on the streets of the capital had been protesting not only against the Imperial Government's conduct of the war but also against the war itself, with all the terrible hardships it had imposed on the lives of the ordinary people. Thus, when the Provisional Government launched further military offensives against the Germans in the summer of 1917, incurring further heavy casualties and reverses for the Russians, the workers of Petrograd again took to the streets in protest, this time against the Provisional Government.

From July onward, the battle-weary soldiers began to 'vote with their feet' by deserting from the front and returning to their native villages to join in the share-out of the gentry's land.

THE BOLSHEVIK REVOLUTION AND THE CIVIL WAR

In this situation, the only party that consistently promised to take Russia immediately out of the war and devote itself to social reform, rather than to the pursuit of military victory, was Lenin's Bolshevik Party. All other major political organisations, including the other socialist parties, the Mensheviks and the Socialist-Revolutionaries (SRs), were pledging to continue the war effort and support the Provisional Government. It was primarily on the basis of their promises of peace and bread that the Bolsheviks were able, in the course of the summer of 1917, gradually to increase their support in the Soviets of Petrograd and Moscow and in other key industrial centres throughout the country.

The Bolshevik Party had played only a minor role in the February Revolution, which was basically a spontaneous outburst of mass unrest. When the autocracy fell in February, the handful of Bolshevik leaders in the capital at that time greeted this event as the long awaited 'bourgeois–democratic revolution' that would usher in a period of parliamentary democracy in Russia; for this reason, they gave qualified support to the Provisional Government. Lenin, however, read the situation differently. The Bolshevik leader had been living in exile in Switzerland during the war; he returned to Russia in April 1917, in a special sealed train made available by the German government for the repatriation of Russian revolutionaries. On his arrival in Petrograd, Lenin declared that the formation of the Workers' and Soldiers' Soviets after February meant that the time was now ripe for the Revolution to pass into its second, socialist stage, and he put forward the slogan 'All Power to the Soviets'.

On Lenin's return to Petrograd in April, the Bolsheviks still had only minority support in the Soviets, which were dominated by the more moderate socialist parties, the Mensheviks and the SRs. In the course of the summer, however, the Mensheviks and SRs steadily lost popularity. In May 1917, they had joined the liberals to form a coalition, and their participation in the Provisional Government, as well as their support for the war, alienated them from the workers and soldiers, whose demands and aspirations were more clearly reflected in the Bolshevik programme.

The Second All-Russia Congress of Soviets of Workers' and Soldiers' Deputies was due to meet in Petrograd on 26 October, and Lenin knew that the Bolsheviks would have a majority in that Congress. On the night of the 25th, armed Bolshevik detachments went into action. Under the direction of the Military Revolutionary Committee of the Petrograd Soviet, led by Trotsky, they implemented a prearranged plan to take over all the key positions in the capital. The operation was virtually bloodless, and the Provisional Government made little attempt to resist. The citizens of Petrograd woke up next morning to find the city in Bolshevik hands. Later that day, the Bolshevik-dominated Congress of Soviets approved Lenin's seizure of power and passed the first two revolutionary decrees of the new Bolshevik government — the decree on peace and the decree on land, which authorised the redistribution of gentry land to the peasantry.

The October seizure of power in Petrograd, however, marked only the beginning of the Bolshevik Revolution in Russia. The Second Congress of Soviets, it is true, had accepted the October Revolution; but this was a Congress of workers' and soldiers' deputies, unrepresentative of the majority of the Russian population, the peasants. The extent to which the Bolsheviks were in a minority in the country as a whole was illustrated dramatically by the elections to the Constituent Assembly that took place in November 1917, a few weeks after the Bolshevik seizure of power. In this general election, the Bolsheviks received only a quarter of the votes cast, whereas the Socialist-Revolutionaries, a rival socialist party with widespread support among the peasants, had an absolute majority of both votes and seats. The Constituent Assembly met once, in January 1918, but when its SR majority came out in opposition to the October Revolution, it was forcibly disbanded by the Bolshevik government. Soon afterwards, civil war broke out in Russia between those who supported the Bolshevik government and those who opposed it. The Civil War dragged on for three years, imposing even greater hardships on the Russian people than those of the World War, which the Bolshevik Revolution had claimed it would bring to an end.

The Civil War resulted in a Bolshevik victory and in the consolidation, by 1921, of the rule of the Soviet government over most of the territory of the former Russian Empire. But the Bolshevik victory in the Civil War did not mean that Lenin enjoyed any more popular support in 1921 than in 1917. The peasantry, in particular, were more hostile to the Soviet government at the end of the Civil War. The Bolsheviks had gained the passive neutrality, if not the active support, of the peasants in 1917 by their decree on the redistribution of the land; but during the Civil War the peasants were antagonised by the Bolshevik policy of requisitioning grain and other foodstuffs from the countryside to feed the towns and the Red Army. Bolshevik support lay in strategically important areas, such as the major industrial centres and the armed forces, and these were the factors that, in the last resort, were to win the Civil War for the Bolsheviks.

CONTROVERSIES ABOUT THE OCTOBER REVOLUTION

The events of 1917 have given rise to major controversies among historians and others about the nature and aims of the Russian Revolution. Much of the discussion turns on the question of the inevitability of Bolshevism. Was the Bolshevik path the only possible way forward for Russia after the collapse of the monarchy in February 1917? Was there any realistic alternative to Bolshevism? For example, what were the chances for the establishment of parliamentary democracy on the Western European model? Had the Bolshevik Revolution not taken place, might not Russia, bearing in mind her tremendous natural resources, have continued to industrialise in a more gradual, if perhaps less spectacular, way while avoiding many of the harsher aspects of Stalinism? Or were there inherent factors in the structure of Russian society that ruled out the possibility of her following the capitalist path of development of Western Europe, under its relatively liberal and democratic parliamentary regimes?

With the benefit of hindsight, one might well argue that the failure of the Provisional Government to come to grips with the problems Russia was facing in 1917 was, in some way, symptomatic of the weakness of the social base that existed for parliamentary democracy in Russia. Incompetent government is not a phenomenon unique to the Russia of 1917. But in most cases incompetent governments are able to muddle through for lack of any viable alternative. In Russia

27

Lenin addresses a crowd in Red Square, Moscow, on the first anniversary of the October Revolution, 1918. (*SCR*)

there was an alternative — the Bolshevik Party, whose leader was courageous, or ruthless, enough to seize power on the basis of a realistic assessment of his own strength and that of the opposition. In taking this decision, Lenin was fortified by his brand of Marxism, which claimed that the 'dictatorship of the proletariat', i.e. political rule by the industrial working class, represented a higher and more progressive form of government than did the formal institutions of parliamentary democracy.

But did the October revolution in practice mean that the workers had come to power? Until quite recently, Western and Soviet historians would have provided rather different answers to this question. Some older Western historians argued that Lenin, through his obedient and well-organised Bolshevik Party, manipulated the ignorant and uneducated working masses to gain power for himself. Soviet historians, by contrast, insisted that the Revolution had genuine popular support, although they also stressed the unique political role of Lenin as an organiser and propagandist. Recent studies by some Western historians, however, suggest that the workers independently reached conclusions about the necessity of Soviet power that corresponded with Lenin's views. They also depict the Bolshevik Party as less centralised and disciplined, more democratic and responsive to pressures from below, than previous writers had implied. This last point is reflected to some extent in the newer Soviet historiography, which is coming to acknowledge that other Bolshevik leaders besides Lenin played important roles in 1917.

The October Revolution, then, was a 'workers' revolution' to the extent that, by the late summer of 1917, most of the industrial working class in the capital and other major industrial centres supported the idea of transferring power to the Soviets. But the seizure of power itself was planned and carried out on behalf of the workers and the Soviets by Lenin and the leaders of the Bolshevik party. Thus we can still argue that the Bolshevik Revolution was the result of specific decisions taken by specific individuals on the basis of Lenin's highly controversial analysis of the revolutionary situation existing in Russia in 1917. Lenin's decision to seize power in October was, as he admitted at the time, a gamble, a calculated risk that paid off insofar as the Bolsheviks were able to retain power.

The fact that the Bolshevik Revolution was successful does not, in itself, prove that the Leninist analysis was correct or that Russia in 1917 was, in any sense, 'ready for socialism'. Lenin himself believed that socialist revolution was required in the rest of Europe before socialism could be built in a backward country like Russia. But socialist revolution failed to emerge from the postwar crisis elsewhere in Europe, and Bolshevism remained isolated. Many of the problems that the Soviet government faced in the ensuing years derived directly from the fact that many of the factors that Marx had declared to be necessary preconditions for the creation of a socialist society (such as the existence of a mature industrial base) were conspicuously absent in the emerging Soviet state, with its predominantly peasant population and an economy ravaged by seven continuous years of war, revolution, and civil war. In the months and years that followed October, the 'dictatorship of the proletariat' increasingly took on the form of a dictatorship by the Bolshevik Party alone. The Bolsheviks had never had the active support of the mass of the peasant population of Russia; even their backing from sections of the working class was to prove short-lived, as conditions in the towns and cities deteriorated during the Civil War of 1918–20. It is difficult to disprove the claims of Soviet historians that the Bolshevik Party (renamed the Communist Party in the spring of 1918) has always enjoyed the support of the masses; but it is significant that, since the dissolution of the Constituent Assembly in January 1918, the Communist Party has never put its claim to popular support to the acid test of free multiparty elections. All parties other than the Communist Party have been outlawed since 1921.

If the Bolshevik Revolution was not inevitable, but rather the consequence of specific decisions taken by specific individuals at a specific moment in time, was it justified? The Bolsheviks in 1917 had only minority support in Russia, but one of their justifications for seizing power was in terms of the benefits that socialism would bring to the people as a whole. You may feel that the seizure of political power by a minority is always wrong and inevitably leads to dictatorship; or you may adopt a more pragmatic position and argue, as Lenin did, that the end justifies the means. In either case, assessment of the Bolshevik Revolution must inevitably be coloured by one's evaluation of the achievements and failures of the Soviet government in the seventy years since the Revolution.

The Soviet reality of today bears little resemblance to the ideal of the just and egalitarian socialist society that inspired so many of the early Bolsheviks with revolutionary enthusiasm. At the same time, the standard of living and the quality of life of the Russian people today, while still lagging well behind the West, are in many respects far better than that of their grandparents and great-grandparents before the First World War. These are the benefits of the Revolution, and insofar as they are real benefits, and not just figments of Soviet propaganda, the Bolsheviks deserve credit for them. The costs, however, were also very great, and insofar as they were the result of a conscious decision by Lenin to impose a one-party dictatorship on the country, the Bolsheviks must also bear the blame.

3

Industrialisation and After

R. W. DAVIES

The Russian economy was devastated by the First World War, and the Civil War and foreign intervention that followed the Revolution of 1917. In 1921, confronted with the hostility of the peasants discussed in the previous chapter, Lenin introduced the New Economic Policy (NEP). This policy allowed the peasants freedom to trade on the market. It also permitted private traders and privately-owned factories on a small scale, and various forms of cooperatives. But factory industry remained in state ownership. This was a mixed economy. On the whole, NEP was successful: by 1927, the production of Soviet farms and factories had more or less regained its prewar level.

The first socialist government in the world now began its heroic effort to undertake the radical reconstruction of Soviet society. The circumstances were somewhat unexpected and highly unfavourable. The founders of world Communism, Marx and Engels, believed that socialism would first be established in an advanced industrial country, but Russia in the mid-1920s was still primarily a peasant country. Only one-sixth of the population of 147 millions lived in the towns; five-sixths still lived in the countryside, and nearly all of these were peasants scratching a living from a land that was parcelled into strips. More than half of them could neither read nor write. Many of them had never travelled beyond their nearest market town.

In the first few years after the Revolution, Lenin and his colleagues continued to believe that the successful construction of a socialist

Lenin at the May Day demonstration, 1919. (*SCR*)

society could be undertaken only in an advanced country. They hoped, therefore, that Soviet Russia would soon be joined by a Soviet Germany, or England, or France. Instead, the Soviet government found itself in power alone. In the mid-1920s, the Left opposition headed by Trotsky within the Soviet Communist Party feared that, as a result of the isolation of the Soviet Union and the apparent dying-out of revolutionary fervour within the Party, there was a serious danger that private capitalism would be restored in Russia. This belief of an important section of the Communist Party was widely shared in the West at the time, and much comfort was drawn from it.

The great economist John Maynard Keynes declared soon after the First World War that the Russian economy could not even get back to its prewar level 'within a reasonable period of time except through the agency of German enterprise and organisation'. In 1926, after a visit to Russia, he announced that there was nothing for the West to learn from Russian planning. In the same year, the present

Lord Boothby, then a young conservative Member of Parliament, who had visited Moscow, stated in the *British–Russian Gazette* that the Soviet regime was gradually evolving toward democracy. An American business visitor optimistically remarked in the same journal:

> Russian business is today in a transition state, passing from a purely Socialistic Government-owned regime to a condition in which Government and private enterprise are becoming more and more inextricably intermingled and intertwined . . . [Russia is] rapidly getting ready to make the transition to a substantial measure of private capitalism.

These prophecies proved to be false, for the Soviet leaders decided to go it alone. They resolved, and were supported in this by a substantial number of the rank and file within the Party, that Russia must undertake an industrial and technical revolution if the standard of living and the culture of her people were to surpass those of the advanced Western countries and thus demonstrate the superiority of socialism. In view of the failure of revolution elsewhere, they would have to do this with Russia's own resources. The task seemed to them an urgent one. They were profoundly conscious that Soviet Russia was isolated in a hostile world and believed that without a strong industrial base for defence the country would be overcome by its foreign enemies, as had happened so often to Tsarist Russia over the centuries.

Stalin summed up this resolve in November 1928, just as he was coming to supreme power:

> In order to achieve the final victory of socialism in our country, it is necessary to catch up and surpass the advanced countries in both a technical and an economic respect. Either we achieve this, or they will destroy us.

INDUSTRIALISATION UNDER STALIN (1925–53)

In the next ten years, Russia underwent a vast industrial expansion, the most rapid and most extensive anywhere in the world up to that time (Fig. 5). So much new industry was started in these years that

Joseph Stalin (*SCR*)

Soviet industrialisation was often compared to sewing a coat on to a button. Millions of unskilled peasants poured into the towns and took on labouring jobs on the building sites and in the new factories; existing towns expanded, and new towns were built. In the early stages, food was very scarce, conditions were generally bad, and the workers were very inefficient. But within a few years, the new workers were 'boiled in the factory kettle', as the Russian saying goes. Within a period of 13 years, between 1926 and 1939, the urban population rose from one-sixth to one-third of the total — from 26 to 56 million people. A vast education programme brought almost universal literacy to a country in which, in 1917, most people could not read and write (see Ch. 10).

These advances were achieved through a system of state planning. As industry and trade were owned and controlled not by private individuals or companies, but by the state, the government was able to concentrate people and materials in key industries to a greater extent than has been possible in peacetime anywhere in the

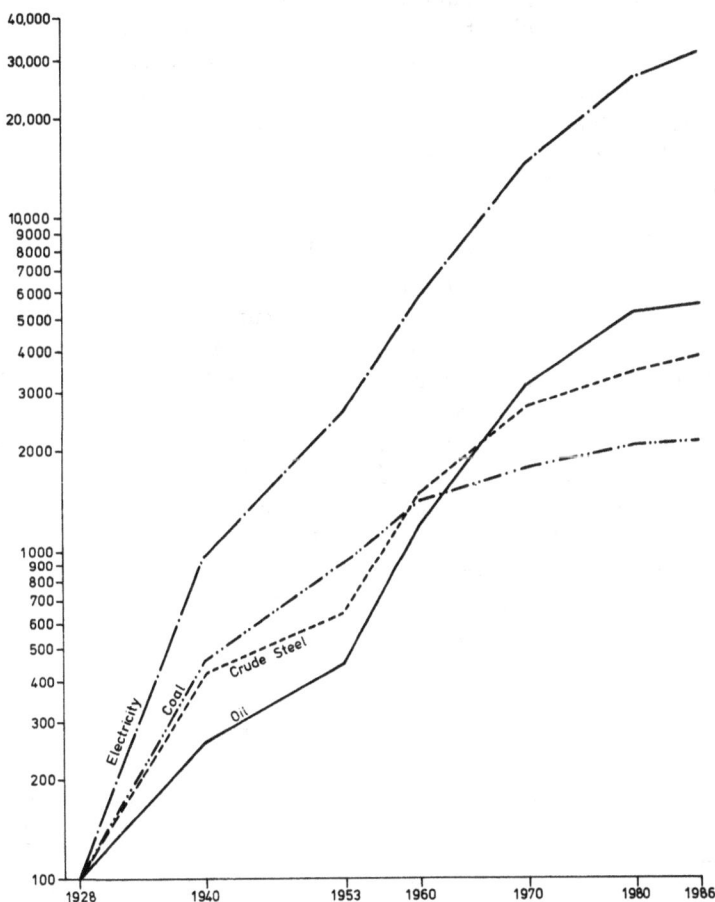

Figure 5   *Industrial Growth in the USSR, 1928–1986*

35

non-Communist world. In some ways, this resembled government planning in Britain during the Second World War; it was a kind of war economy.

Whereas control over industry was brought about relatively easily, the relationship between the Bolsheviks and the peasants presented problems of extreme difficulty. The bringing together of more than 100 million peasants into cooperative farms had always been a goal of the Bolsheviks. Cooperation plus the use of modern machinery was supposed to transform the peasant economy. In the long run, such a transformation did occur. But in the short term the government was preoccupied with the urgent problem of obtaining food for the growing towns. The Soviet government had little to offer the peasants in the way of consumer goods in exchange for their grain and meat. First priority was being given to the coal mines, steel mills, machine tools, and other heavy industries, which form the basis for the industrial development of a modern nation, and little or nothing was left to increase the production of consumer goods to raise the standard of living immediately. The Soviet leaders did not have much experience in the kind of economic manoeuvring required to get the best out of this situation, and they made serious blunders in handling it. Under these circumstances, the peasantry were most reluctant to part with their grain. A friend of the author, who was active in Russian politics in the late 1920s, argued that the stormy political controversies that were rocking the Russian Communists all resulted from the annual grain crisis: every year the state tried to get grain and other foodstuffs from the peasantry, and every year its failure to do so led to fierce disputes among the politicians as to what should be done about it. There were very few Russian Communists who were willing to admit, in public at any rate, the extent of the difficulties they faced and the severity of the measures that would be needed if industrialisation was going to succeed.

By the end of 1927, the pressures of industrialisation, coupled with a few blunders, had resulted in a particularly severe crisis in food supplies. This brought about a dramatic change: it was one of those moments of choice in which the whole aspect of a nation's life is altered. Stalin was in a strong position. He had defeated Trotsky and his group in 1927 and became the almost undisputed master of the Communist Party. He and his supporters now came down firmly on the side of industrialisation at all costs. Capitalist countries, Stalin argued, had been able to industrialise in the past

The metallurgical combine 'Stalin' in Kuznetsk, 1933. (*SCR*)

only by exploiting their colonies and their own workpeople or, in some cases, by getting loans from other countries. If Russia was to industrialise on her own resources, she would have to get more out of her peasantry. Stalin's policy met with strong but unsuccessful opposition from some of his fellow Communists. This 'right-wing' opposition, which included the principal trade union and government leaders, was led by Bukharin, the most prominent Communist intellectual, who wanted to slow down industrialisation and appease the peasants. Bukharin argued that Stalin's policy must involve the development of something like a police state and the return to War Communism, and that it threatened the fate of the whole revolution. Stalin also anticipated that his policy would involve opposition among peasants and others, but he believed that this could be curbed by a very firm hand.

Historians still argue whether Stalin's accomplishments were a betrayal of the Revolution or a necessary consolidation of it. At all events, what happened in the next few years was far more drastic and brutal than Bukharin had feared and Stalin anticipated. In 1930–1 the majority of peasants were persuaded, cajoled, or bullied into

37

Stalin poses with peasant women in an apparently relaxed mood, 1935. (*SCR*)

joining the new collective farms, at a time when only a trickle of machinery was available to work the collective land. The more prosperous peasants, or *kulaks* (the Russian word for tight fist), and those who showed too much opposition, several million persons in all, were summarily and often brutally exiled from their villages because they were believed to be a political danger. In his famous novel, *Virgin Soil Upturned*, Sholokhov described vividly how a local poor peasants' committee confiscated the house, the farm animals, the iron bedstead and eiderdown, the crockery, and even the concertina of the richest local family and expelled them from their village. The army and the political police were often called in to drive out the kulaks and force the peasants into collectives. Fodder for farm animals was scarce, and many peasants killed and ate their livestock rather than put it in the common pool. As a result, agricultural production fell considerably, and famine resulted in 1932–3. Millions died.

Bitter feelings about collectivisation still linger in Russia. Some Soviet and many Western historians believe that the damage it caused was far greater than the gains. But the new collective farm system enabled the government to obtain at least a minimum of foodstuffs for the rapidly growing town population: the collective farms under Communist control handed over much more grain to the state than peasant smallholders would have been willing to part with voluntarily, though other kinds of food supplies declined. The upheavals and hunger of the early 1930s were the terrible price paid by the Russian countryfolk so that rapid industrialisation could be forced through; this is not to say, however, that this policy was the most sensible way of coping with the problem.

During the remainder of the 1930s, agriculture slowly recovered to the 1928 level, as farm machinery poured in eventually from the towns and the peasants became somewhat more reconciled to the new system.

In all these developments, the Communist Party, with Stalin at its head, played a unique part. The way the Communist Party — Russians in conversation refer to it as the Party — fits into Soviet life is one of the most difficult things to grasp. For the Russian Party member, the Party was, as it were, church and political party and masonic lodge rolled into one; for the Russian non-Party person, for the Russian people as a whole, the Party with its couple of million members was, in the 1930s, the driving motor of the whole industrialisation process. The history of the Party is discussed further in Chapter 4; here we consider its role, and the role of its leader Stalin, in the industrialisation drive. Stalin's competence as a politician may perhaps be measured by his success in moulding the Party into an instrument to guide an industrialisation that was being carried out by a Russian state, with all its historical traditions. Stalin also played an important part in providing the Party with a set of views that have become known as 'Stalinism'. One function of Stalinism was to provide justifications or excuses for the repressive policies of the 1930s; but it was also, in my view, an adaptation of Marxism, which made it more capable of inspiring and prodding the Party member in the work of building a new Russia. In a Russian novel (Dudintsev's *Not by Bread Alone*), published a few years after Stalin's death, the self-made factory manager who has risen to power as one of the new men of the industrialisation period has a copy of Stalin's little textbook, *Dialectical and Historical Materialism*, as his bedside book, and he annoys his wife by reading extracts to her to justify his rather selfish conduct as an official and as a man. This use of a philosophical textbook by a typical key figure in Russian society is, perhaps, a tribute to the pervasiveness, if nothing else, of Stalin's political philosophy.

A god-like Stalin at the head of the Party acted as the pivot of the Communist Party machine and the inspirer of the hundreds of thousands of Party members who went out, on Party instructions, to establish firm control over the collective farms and to build new towns in the backwoods. There was no place in Stalin's Party for the dissenter; the political police were on the watch, and the labour camp awaited the unwise critic. Under Stalin's management, the intellectuals who had held many of the top offices in the first years after the Revolution were thrust aside, often not very gently, by ex-workers and others who were aspiring to high positions. The disciplined body of Party men that ran Russia's new farms and factories was worlds apart from the relatively amorphous Party of revolutionaries in 1917.

Thus the political and economic system established in the early 1930s, which continued until Stalin's death and after, was one in which the state owned and controlled most of the economy, planned its growth, and pushed industrialisation ruthlessly and relentlessly. The state itself was controlled by the Communist Party with Stalin at its head. The Party elite formed part of a wider social group of professional and administrative personnel, which was as a whole the leading section of the townsmen. This system enabled the establishment of a powerful industry that formed the backbone of Russia's military strength and enabled her to resist successfully the onslaught of the German invasion between 1941 and 1945. The impact of this invasion was devastating, and human suffering was immense. At least 20 million Soviet citizens were killed or died prematurely; much of Soviet industry was destroyed. But after 1945 recovery was rapid.

By the time of Stalin's death in 1953, Russia had almost completely recovered from the devastation of the Second World War and was firmly established as the second most advanced military power.

RESULTS OF INDUSTRIALISATION

Soviet industrialisation, then, was a system of forced economic development that carried with it enormous economic and some social benefits on the one hand and enormous costs and sacrifices on the other hand. It was able to concentrate resources successfully on major projects, catching up with the United States in the hydrogen bomb race in 1953 and launching the world's first satellite in 1957. This centralised system facilitated the rapid introduction into the USSR of the most advanced technological processes from the United States and elsewhere, brought about great economies of scale in production, and provided, through the centralised production drive, a spur for management and men to work harder in the common cause. Great losses occurred, however, partly due to the concentration of effort on the priority sectors, so that the others were starved, and partly due to the bureaucratic system associated with it. The destruction of livestock and the decline in peasant morale were counterparts of the triumphs in heavy industry. The lack of initiative and innovation at the works level was a consequence of the concentration of economic power in the hands of the central authorities. There is a great deal of controversy among historians and social scientists about whether these losses and failures were due primarily to the nature of the Soviet system itself, to economic necessity, to special Russian or Soviet historical circumstances, or perhaps even to the unfortunate nature of Stalin's personality. Some people say that you can't make an omelette without breaking eggs; the Stalinist system was a package deal, and the losses were a function of the gains. But it is clear that to a great extent the historical past of the Tsarist autocracy and the inexperience and imperfect knowledge of the people who brought the first planned economy into being drove the system away from its optimum, even in terms of the goal of forced industrialisation.

A judicious assessment of this Soviet experience is of great importance. The industrialisation of the Soviet Union, and the form that it took under Stalin, has had profound consequences for both Russia and the world at large. Any visitor to present-day Russia is immediately struck by the contrast between old and new, which is a direct result of the industrialisation process. Even nowadays, when you spend some time in a Russian town, especially in the provinces, you feel as if you are watching a scene from one of Maxim Gorky's novels about pre-Revolutionary days, but with large chunks of modern America somehow mixed up with it: old women in shawls jostle the young men with briefcases on dilapidated buses and up-to-date metros and hovercraft. Stalin created a Russia in which the most modern blast furnaces in the world could be found side by side with overcrowded housing conditions that, at the time of his

Constructing the Chelyabinsk Tractor Works during the early five-year plans. Construction in the early period often relied on primitive techniques and mass labour. (*SCR*)

death, had not improved much since the Revolution; a Russia in which government policy was already aimed at raising the school-leaving age to the very high level of 17-plus, but in which many of the shopping facilities and everyday goods that the British housewife takes for granted were completely absent.

Soviet industrialisation was also important because of the influence it exercised on the rest of the world. In some ways, it seemed to teach the rest of the world what not to do. The Communist Parties in the West lost much support because they were identified with the purges, the inhumanities, and the social inequalities that formed part of the Communist or the Stalinist version of socialism. But the ability of the Soviet state to produce a dynamic economic system exercised a profound influence on Western economic thinking. Remember that the years of Russia's great industrial advances were the years of the Great Depression in the West.

The first Pelican book to deal with economics, Pelican No. 7, published in 1937 and written by G. D. H. Cole, a prominent British Labour Party economist, was primarily devoted to contrasting Soviet and Western economic development in the previous ten years. His graphs of France, Britain, Germany, Italy, and above all the United States, showed the great decline after 1928 (Figs. 6 & 7). In the United States, industrial production fell by more than 40 per cent, building activity by four-fifths, and factory employment by one-third. In the same period, in spite of all the privations described, Soviet industry boomed; large-scale unemployment vanished. This boom played an important part in influencing the movement in favour of state planning in the democratic Western countries in the 1930s and during the Second World War. It was undoubtedly a factor in the emergence of the mixture of state control and private ownership that was characteristic of most Western industrial countries in the first thirty years or so after the Second World War.

Soviet industrialisation has also exercised a major influence on the four-fifths of the world that is not yet industrialised. Soviet success convinced them that it was possible in a comparatively short time for a relatively backward country to become advanced, to leap into the 20th century. The great developments in China — for all their quarrels with the Russians — were inspired by Soviet success; this

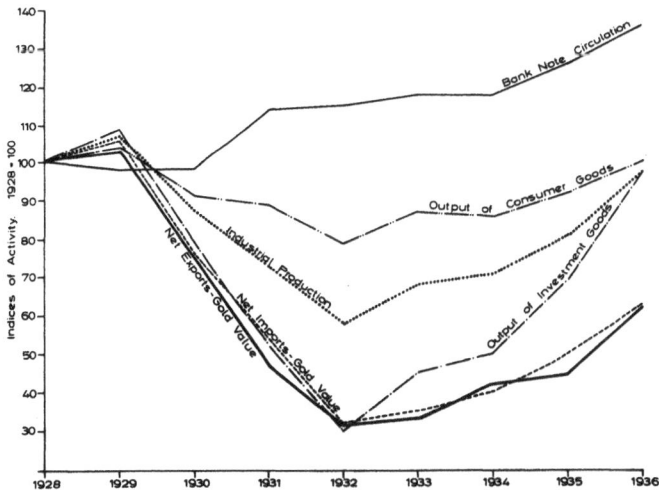

Figure 6   *Economic Activity in the United States, 1928–1936*

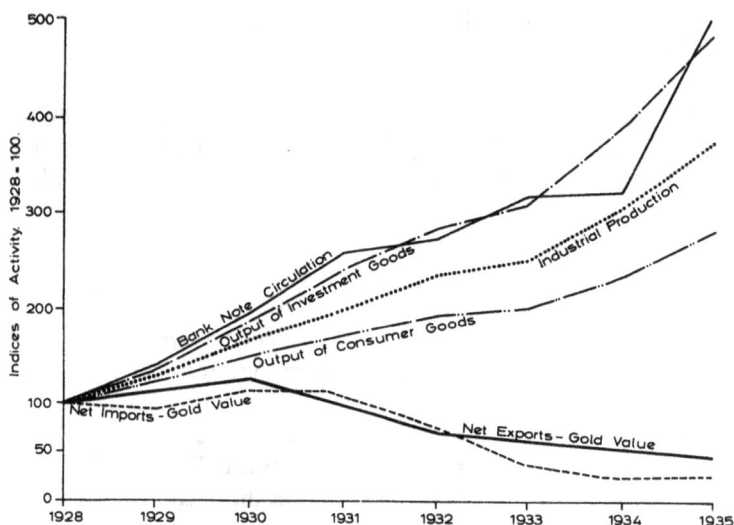

Figure 7   *Economic Activity in the USSR, 1928–1935*

success has also provided a yardstick against which the economic failures or successes of ex-colonial nations tend to be measured. Perhaps from the vantage point of AD 2100, Soviet industrialisation will be seen primarily as a crucial stage in spreading the process of economic and social transformation, which began in England in the middle of the 18th century, to the thousands of millions of peasants who now live on the borders of starvation.

THE SOVIET ECONOMY SINCE STALIN

In the decades since Stalin's death, a new set of issues has come to the forefront. If the Soviet system of government was successful in pulling a fairly backward country up by its bootstraps, can it be equally successful in coping with the problems of an industrialised country? The Soviet economy nowadays is radically different from that in which central planning by administrative order was introduced in the 1920s. The traditional pattern of distribution of the national income has proved difficult to maintain; Soviet planners have come under strong pressure, to which they have partly yielded, to raise the standard of living by transferring resources to agriculture and to the consumer goods and service industries. At the same time, the desire to overtake the United States economically and to equal it in military potential has put an immense strain on resources.

This is the economic background to the changes in the planning system in the past 30 years. The pressure on resources has led the Soviet leaders to pin great hopes on increased economic efficiency; and the drive for increased efficiency is at the centre of the reforms in economic planning that have been undertaken in recent years. By the 1950s, it had become increasingly difficult to improve economic efficiency within the framework of a highly centralised planning system.

Two factors are at work here. First, as Soviet technology progresses, technical advances in an increasing number of industries can no longer be achieved merely by adapting to Soviet conditions technology that has been borrowed from advanced industrial countries. Further progress depends much more on innovations within the Soviet Union itself. Second, the Soviet economy is vastly more complex than it was in the 1920s. In 1926, total Soviet industrial production was no greater than the production of one of the largest United States industrial companies. But Soviet industrial production is now more than half that of the United States, and the production of armaments roughly equals the U.S. level.

The need for technical innovation and the greater complexity of the economy both point to the need to devolve the decision-making powers of the central authorities and to devise a more flexible system of planning that is easier to administer. Such a devolution of power would also make it possible to provide more scope for the initiative of the new professional classes. Here is a major potential source of improved efficiency. To quote one striking example: in 1928, the total number of qualified engineers employed in the Soviet economy was 47 000; in 1950, the number had increased to 400 000; by 1985, it had reached 6 058 000 — 129 times as many as in 1928. Taking all these points together, the history of Soviet planning since the death of Stalin may perhaps be interpreted as an attempt to find a solution that would combine flexibility and greater initiative throughout the system with the retention, by the central planners, of the powers that have often brought the Soviet economy success in its major priorities.

Four major efforts to reform planning have been made since 1953. Between 1954 and 1956, an attempt was made, within the existing

45

administrative hierarchy, to transfer decision-making powers systematically to lower rungs in the hierarchy (from Council of Ministers and Gosplan to industrial ministry, from ministry to factory) and to cut the number of centrally approved targets and instructions. In 1957, this attempt was abandoned in favour of the decision to reorganise industry on a regional basis; 104 regional councils (*sovnarkhozy*), each in charge of all factories in their region, replaced the thirty ministries that had each been responsible for a sector of industry for the whole country. Eight years later, in the 'Kosygin reform' of September 1965, this attempt was relinquished, and the ministries were restored. Together with this a serious but ultimately unsuccessful effort was made to increase greatly the importance of the profit motive as a regulator of the economic behaviour of industrial firms. The political aspects of these reforms are discussed in Chapter 5.

After a series of minor attempts at reform in the course of two decades after 1965, a fourth economic reform, much more far-reaching than its predecessors, was launched in June 1987; its first stage to take effect in the following three years. This 1987 reform is examined in Chapter 7.

The road ahead for the Soviet economy is a difficult one that will undoubtedly have many twists and turns. If the 1987 reforms succeed, this success could overshadow the Soviet achievement in pioneering the large-scale national planning of rapid industrialisation. This would not only make it possible for the Soviet Union to achieve the goal set by Soviet policy in 1928, to catch up and surpass the advanced capitalist economies, but would also greatly increase the collective control by human beings over their own future. If the 1987 reforms fail like the previous reforms, or are not successful enough, the Soviet economic system will be judged historically as one that proved able to cope, at great human cost, with the first stages of industrialisation in a developing country, but could not deal with the problems of economic growth and technical change in a more advanced industrial society.

4

The Communist Party,
Yesterday and Today

M. LEWIN

LENIN'S CONCEPT OF THE PARTY

An understanding of the history and functions of the Soviet Communist Party is crucial to an understanding of the contemporary Soviet Union. This is a complicated theme that could be approached from many different angles and standpoints. Here we consider the contemporary Party in relation to the concept of the Party and the blueprint for social revolution that were developed by Lenin, the founder of the Party, before 1917.

Lenin's plan for revolution and social reorganisation had at least two major aspects, represented by his two famous publications: *What Is to Be Done?*, written in 1902, and *State and Revolution*, written a month before he took power in 1917.

In *What Is to Be Done?*, Lenin dealt primarily with organisational and strategic questions. He argued that to overthrow the Tsarist regime a special type of revolutionary organisation must be created: 'Give us an organisation of revolutionaries, and we will overturn Russia!' He regarded such an organisation as essential because spontaneous popular movements would not, in themselves, bring about a new socialist order of society. In Lenin's view, the factory working class, which had come into being in Russia with the emergence of modern industry, would fight for its own day-to-day interests but would not on its own initiative go beyond a reformist struggle for better conditions. Socialism had to be brought to the working class from outside, and in Russian conditions this could only be done by an organisation of professional revolutionaries, trained to operate in illegal conditions and capable of out-

47

Lenin and other party members at the IX Congress in 1920. (*Alfred A. Knopf, Inc.; Wildwood House Ltd.*)

manoeuvring the Tsarist political police with their network of informers. These professional revolutionaries would analyse the whole social and political structure of Tsarist society and on this basis hammer out the strategy and tactics of the revolutionary movement.

In the conditions of illegality in which it had to work, the internal organisation of the revolutionary party had to be tight, highly centralised and disciplined, and directed toward effective political action. At the same time, the Party had to be capable of analysing society and politics. It would therefore have to be disciplined but flexible: neither a bureaucracy nor a democracy.

This revolutionary party would lead the mass of the people to an armed uprising against autocracy, first replacing autocracy by democracy and then advancing, together with the successful social revolutions in other countries, toward the establishment of a socialist 'dictatorship of the proletariat' (see pp. 79–80 below).

In *State and Revolution*, 15 years later, Lenin set out the purposes of this dictatorship. Lenin outlined the way forward to liberation with a capital *L*, the liberation of society from oppression. The exploitation of one class by another, which had characterised all previous societies, would be eliminated; the division of society into classes would cease to exist. The state, with all its coercive and repressive machinery — armies, police, law courts and bureaucracy — would wither away. In the new system, it would not be difficult for society to run its affairs; every cook, Lenin dreamed, would learn to govern. Government, in any case, would consist of running things, not ruling people. This was a long-established idea among socialists, a dream about a dictatorship that would end dictatorships for all time and establish a society resembling one long advocated by anarchists as well as socialists.

Lenin's organisational blueprint in *What Is to Be Done?* proved to be a great success. Between 1902 and 1917, three revolutions shook Russia, and on 8 November 1917, Lenin, now leader of the triumphant Bolshevik Party, announced: 'We will now proceed to construct the socialist order'. There are few parallel cases in history of events conforming to a carefully drafted action plan, thought up years in advance and then carried out more or less as expected.

Lenin's blueprint for the new social order in *State and Revolution*, on the other hand, was a failure. The Party reached power as Lenin wanted it to. But, 70 years later, it is in charge of a powerful bureaucratic state, something Lenin believed would not continue to exist. The story of the Soviet Union can be seen as the story of the great success and the great failure of Lenin's different blueprints or plans. Why one plan succeeded and one failed is not yet fully understood by historians. But the answer to the question can partly be found by studying the transformation that took place in the Party after 1917.

THE TRANSFORMATION OF THE PARTY, 1917–87

At the beginning of 1917, the Party had at most 20000 members. When it took power later in 1918, membership had increased to about 200000. Today it has well over 17 million members and probationary members.

In 1917, it had no formal administrative machinery. Its committees contained the leading members, and they personally carried out all the political and administrative work. Today the Party is run by an elaborate network of full-time officials, an hierarchically organised Party machine employing some 200000 persons.

Between November 1917 and 1987, the Party has undergone a profound transformation. Seven main stages can be traced.

(1) Before 1917, both the central leadership and the journals of the Bolsheviks, who until 1912 constituted one fraction within the Russian Social-Democratic Party, were located abroad. They therefore had to transmit theories and instructions to the Russian Party from outside. Within Russia, there was a network of illegal committees, each surrounded by groups of sympathisers. But these were not simple soldiers carrying out orders. Leading members from within Russia attended congresses and conferences abroad, and the central committee members in exile, including Lenin, had to fight for and reassert their prestige at every major turning point in the political and ideological discussions. The leading members within Russia enjoyed a considerable degree of independence on many issues, though they tended to look to the leaders in exile, especially Lenin, for guidance on grand theory and major problems of strategy.

(2) In the months between the two revolutions of February and October 1917, enormous changes occurred. The Party suddenly became a legal, mass-opposition Party. It had powerful leadership, which was on the whole followed by the local Party organisations. But these local Party groups continued to enjoy a high degree of autonomy in local affairs; also, through their delegates to the frequent conferences and congresses, they acted as arbiters between quarrelling leaders and participated in the intensive political debates inside the Party. The Party leaders appealed to the rank and file at large and to the local militants in particular to gain approval for their proposals.

(3) From the moment of their victory, and during the Civil War that followed in 1918–20, the Bolsheviks were no longer a revolutionary Party in opposition but virtually the sole holders of political power. This momentous change, and the gigantic effort of winning the Civil War, began to shape the Party in new and different directions. The semi-anarchistic and often unruly Party rank and file began to be moulded into a disciplined, more strictly centralised, militarised organisation. A central Party machine began to emerge. The Politburo was set up to centralise everyday decisions. Secretar-

ies were allocated from the centre, without any form of election, to strengthen local Party cells engaged in propping up the war effort, often justified solely by emergency conditions. Debate and dissent within the Party were restrained because of the need for wartime unity; but debate never stopped, and no obvious efforts to suppress it were undertaken.

(4) After the end of the Civil War, with the introduction of the New Economic Policy (NEP) in 1921 (described in Ch. 3), internal Party debate flared up again.

Up to his death, Lenin's leadership was based on his enormous prestige, and within the Party his was neither a personal nor an authoritarian dictatorship. In the Central Committee of the Party, and in the smaller Politburo, no important decision was taken without a majority vote. Party conferences and congresses were regularly and frequently convened and played an important role in political life. The intermediate ranks in the Party, and even its rank and file, were informed and consulted about major issues. The Party press was lively and well informed and was frank about most of the sensitive issues.

There were, however, some large clouds in this bright sky. At the beginning of NEP, Lenin feared that the Party was in danger of being overthrown by a peasant uprising. Together with the banning of other political parties, Lenin secured the banning of 'fractions and groupings' within the Party. Discussion and criticism of policies would continue, but no concerted presentation of rival programmes was permitted, and, once a decision was taken, disciplined unity was required to carry it out. Whether this was merely intended as a temporary emergency measure or reflected a profound trend within Bolshevism is a hotly disputed question.

(5) At first, the ban on 'fractions and groupings' remained largely on paper. Even after Lenin's death in 1924, opposition groups continued to function within the Party. But a clear trend now emerged toward what was known among all the oppositions as the 'bureaucratisation' of the Party, and it soon became dominant. More and more power was concentrated in the hands of the rapidly expanding Party machine and its leadership, at the expense of the rank and file of the Party and the different political and intellectual interest groups inside and outside the Party. An entirely new aim began to be presented as being the essence of Leninism: the establishment of a 'monolithic' party, which was to be not merely a

51

The 'Industrial Party Trial', November 1930. This trial of prominent engineers on accusations of wrecking was a prelude to the public trials of Party leaders later in the decade. (*R T Hulton*)

party disciplined in action but also one in which any possibility of internal opposition would be stamped out and all criticism eliminated.

(6) By 1930, the monolithic Party was more or less fully established, but its emergence involved a cataclysm. In the purges, especially during the Great Purge of 1936–38, most of the leading Party members were killed, and so were all the previous traditions. An entirely new organisation replaced the earlier revolutionary Party. It was organised on a different basis: the Party machine was fully in command, all Party institutions lost their influence, and the rank and file and lower- and medium-level officials were completely excluded from policy making. It was led in a different way — the group of leaders dominated by Lenin was now replaced by the personal dictatorship of Stalin. The Party was effectively transformed into a ruling bureaucracy in which obedience became the key virtue for all Party members at every level.

Trotsky, opponent of Stalin, exiled from the USSR in 1929. (*RT Hulton*)

The Party had long been seen by its members and leaders as a unique historical instrument for the transformation of society, to which obedience was owed. Even Trotsky, an independent leader of great intellect, frequently asserted that no individual, however talented, could be right against the Party. This treatment of the Party as a fetish or an idol exacted a paradoxical retribution. During the domination of Stalin, the problem of whether or not an individual could be right against the Party vanished. Now the whole Party could never be right against an individual, its leader, who was treated as infallible. The new principle was enforced by terror, but the Party had already been drugged into apathy during the preceding years, with the help of the philosophy that individuals should abdicate their political freedom to an organisation.

(7) Developments since Stalin's death in 1953 are not easy to assess, but it is clear that in the hectic Khrushchev years (1957–64)

Bukharin with Lenin's sister on the editorial staff of *Pravda* in May 1924. Bukharin, a leading member of the Bolshevik Party, was executed after a public trial in March 1938. (*R T Hulton*)

and under Brezhnev (1964–82) and his successors, many new features have emerged.

First, the old style of leadership is gone, and the Party is led by a group of top leaders, members of the Politburo. The introduction of what in Soviet terminology is referred to as a 'collective leadership' is a very real and important change.

Second, much more influence and say are given to the 400-strong Central Committee that fell into abeyance under Stalin. Together with the Central Committee members, there is a group of leading Party officials who also seem to have become an independent political force. Thus, though leadership at the very top is powerful, the ruling group is not just a caucus but a much larger body. Some even use the terms *elite* or *class* to describe this ruling group, which may also include top government officials ánd some social groups, like leading scientists, who have access to the central authorities.

Third, the middle ranks in the Party and the educated public generally now have more say in Party policy. There is much less secrecy than before, more information is made available, and more consultation takes place before policy decisions are made. Policy makers have recently begun to make considerable use of sociological surveys.

Does this mark a fundamentally new stage in the development of the Party? To answer this question, we need to examine the contemporary operation of the Soviet Party in more detail.

THE POLITICAL SYSTEM TODAY

The distinctive feature of the Soviet political system is that it is a one-party system. The ruling party has an undisputed monopoly of power. In Western countries, and particularly in the United States, the one-party system came to be seen, especially during the Cold War, as the embodiment of all that is evil in politics. The origins of the one-party system were traced to Lenin's *What Is to Be Done?*, and some saw the whole thing as a kind of conspiracy by Lenin. Once the Cold War subsided, however, it became easier for observers to perceive that the one-party system was not just the product of one mind, one movement, or one country, but was a genuine creation of history. One-party systems have appeared in all kinds of countries, with all kinds of attributes and labels. We can nowadays study a

E. Ligachev   E. Shevardnadze

N. Slyunkov   A. Yakovlev

Some leading members of Gorbachev's Politburo, 1988.

56

whole range of one-party systems. Some are important instruments of economic and social development, some are instruments of destruction, and some are both at different periods of their development. Some exhibit liberal or democratic tendencies; others degenerate into oppressive machines manipulated by despots. Matters are much more complicated than might have been supposed, especially as we can also observe some democratic processes degenerating in established democracies. To understand the Soviet Communist Party, we evidently need to examine it as one specific case in a variety of one-party systems.

Perhaps the central feature of the Soviet Party, like other Communist Parties, is that it has an official ideology that it imposes on society. This ideology, 'Marxism-Leninism', claims monopoly of ideological life and enforces it as far as it can. Purporting to possess the capacity to formulate a scientific theory of history, society, and even philosophy (though some of these claims are, in practice, somewhat diluted today), the Party considers itself the 'guide' for the whole of Soviet society. 'Guide' could, of course, mean different things in different circumstances. The Soviet Party is not concerned merely with formulating ideology, but also with making policy; indeed, it frequently not only supervises the implementation of policies but also implements them directly. It is thus both a governmental party and a *party-government*; its top leadership is, in fact, responsible for central government, and its intermediate agencies guide the local government. In addition, the scope of Party policy making is enormous. National economic planning, education, culture, and arts — the whole range of social phenomena — are all officially claimed to fall into the Party's purview. Such a party, if it actually does what it claims (and so far this is still the case), can be seen as an agency of comprehensive social planning, shaping, or trying to shape, social forces according to its conceptions and objectives.

What are the main instruments and methods by which the Party carries out this vast range of functions?

First, the enforcement of a monopoly ideology was, and to a point still is, a powerful instrument for securing a high degree of uniformity of views in society. At the same time, it provides a common language between the masses and their rulers and a common frame of reference for the rulers and the different influential groups or elites.

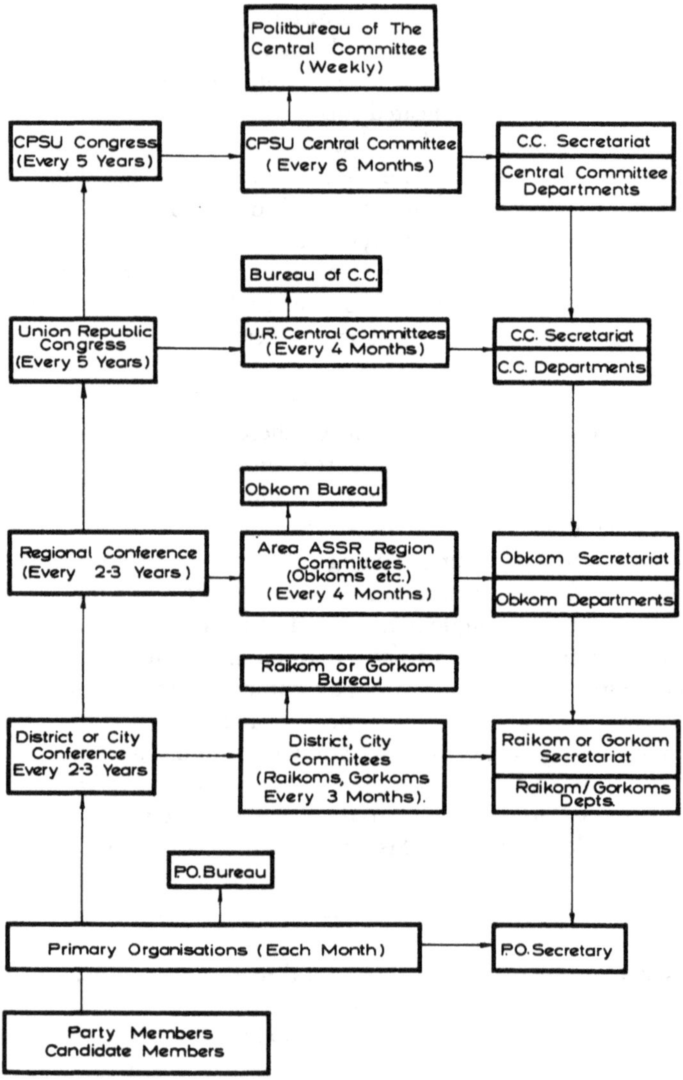

Figure 8   *Structure of the Soviet Communist Party*

Second, all the leading personnel throughout the USSR — people in positions of responsibility in government, science, trade unions, and so on — are trained by the Party or under its supervision and selected for their posts by the Party authorities.

Third, the whole nation is being educated and heavily propagandised under the control of or by the Party (see Ch. 10). The monopoly on power and ideology is supplemented by the monopoly on means of communication and information. Discordant voices in matters seen by the Party as sensitive have a very difficult time, and the whole of politics and ideology comes into this category. Dissenters are often persecuted, the authorities even resorting to the convenient device of locking them away in lunatic asylums.

Fourth, cultural activities, especially art and literature, have to follow prescribed paths and are supervised by powerful censors (see Ch. 11).

Fifth, the Party is organised to enable it to control the governmental machinery and, either through it or, when necessary, directly, the whole of social life. The central leadership, the Politburo, is elected by and formally responsible to the Central Committee, which includes all the leading officials of the Party, the government, and the other most important organisations. The Politburo has at its disposal the Secretariat of the Central Committee, which is organised like a miniature government, with departments responsible for supervising the main branches of industry, culture and science, the police and the army, propaganda, and education. Thus, ministers are supervised by parallel departments in the Central Committee, although the Premier and his two deputies are themselves Politburo members. The Central Committee departments also control the Party itself, with its ubiquitous network of Party primary organisations in every factory, office, or school (see Fig. 8).

Finally, the social composition of the Party membership is regulated to ensure that different classes of society are represented in it in proportions considered appropriate by the central authorities. In particular, citizens of talent and position either reach leading positions because they are Party members or are asked to join because they can be influential among their peers.

All these are impressive political organisational methods that help the Party to run the country, to raise it to a high position in world affairs, and to create a powerful, viable system, though very different from what Lenin's *State and Revolution* anticipated.

So much for the secrets of the Party's success. Let us briefly review some sources of tension and failure. In fact, some factors that made for success are also creating trouble. The one-party monopoly and the very insistence of the leadership on ideological and political unity have both been major sources of trouble. All rulers probably prefer a situation in which they can afford not to suppress all kinds of anarchic, irresponsible opponents and feel free to devise their policies without interruption. But the strong, disciplined Party machinery, shaped by the years of forced industrialisation and world war, is now faced with a new, diversified, complex and quickly changing society. This complexity of the social body cannot be evaded. The purges carried out 50 years ago by a capricious ruler, who wished to eliminate political risks for himself stemming from diversity, cannot easily be repeated today.

So, unavoidably, pressure groups are being formed that have to be accommodated at least to a certain extent. As shown in relation to Soviet culture in Chapter 11, diversity is a reality in spite of police surveillance and powerful censors and controllers. Uniformity of thought just does not exist in the Soviet Union, and the leaders are aware of it. Careful observation shows the existence of different and competing political trends of different denominations, which cannot express themselves freely, but constitute subterranean currents and also penetrate the Party. So far, the Party clings to its monolithic conceptions and is not ready to permit the emergence of different political groups even within the Party itself. It is, therefore, inadequately equipped to deal with political diversity and strife and has to find ways to adapt itself. The pretence of political uniformity is as detrimental to political development as enforced cultural and artistic uniformity is to culture and art. In the field of sciences, some of them extremely sensitive to economic and military development, the sheer need for survival as a state forced the leaders, even before Gorbachev took office in March 1985, to abandon narrow-minded claims; to progress in physics, biology, cybernetics and mathematical economics, the state had to relinquish cherished practices. In the 1970s, some social sciences were still the victim of ideological stifling, but a modern society cannot be run adequately without training its leading personnel to search for solutions to political and social problems in a spirit of independence. Sociology, therefore, had to be allowed, even during the restrictive political atmosphere of the later Brezhnev years, when strong efforts were made to keep it

60

from overstepping the limits of a practical, problem-solving technique. But it is only cultural diversity, intellectual and political challenge, and a free flow of information that allow both the development of sciences and the training of open-minded elites and leaders. During the Brezhnev period, there was growing pressure on the Party for access to ever more information in different fields, without which the complex process of training leading personnel is constantly hampered.

The Soviet system has entered a stage in which it will bear many pressures for change and is on a threshold of important transformations. Is the straitjacket put on society by political institutions really unbearable and crisis-laden? What will be the eventual direction of political change? Is there a channel for democratic change within the Soviet political system? Are there Soviet forms of democracy that could emerge within the framework of a one-party system?

These issues form the background to the spate of reforms since Gorbachev became General Secretary of the Party in March 1985. Behind these hectic changes is the remarkable development of Soviet society that has occurred in the last three decades. The most potent mainspring of this change was the process of urbanisation. The ratio of rural to urban population, about two to one on the eve of the war, is now almost reversed. An essentially rural society is now essentially urban — an entirely new situation in the whole of Russian history. The momentous results of this social turnabout are now unfolding. A new class structure, a new professional profile for the whole population, with higher standards of education for everyone, and a greatly expanded professional, scientific and artistic 'intelligentsia' — all these and many other factors press hard on the political system and compel the leaders of Party and state to face a different reality and handle problems in new ways. Obviously, the composition of the Party and the character and quality of its leadership reflect the complexity of urban society. Bureaucrats and leaders are themselves part of the intelligentsia, aware of its moods and needs, dependent on experts, and responsive to public opinion, which is a new and potent fact in Soviet political life. Hence, the cascade of changes that concern not just the economy but also the sphere of culture, the way of ruling, and the whole political discourse. Hence, also, a chain of reforms in most branches of administration, especially in the Party itself. The object of rule — Soviet urban society — is now entirely different from what the Tsars, Lenin,

Stalin, and even Khrushchev had to face. The subject of rule — the Communist Party — is being thoroughly transformed. The depth of these transformations is an object of struggle of considerable intensity, but we can conclude that they cannot be blocked for too long, nor can they be reversed.

5

Soviet Politics:
Perspectives and Prospects

RONALD AMANN

THE STALINIST LEGACY

The death of Joseph Stalin in March 1953 marked the end of a stormy and violent chapter in Soviet history, yet the reverberations of his rule are still felt in the Soviet Union to this day. Indeed, Soviet politics during the past 35 years can be seen as a series of attempts by Stalin's successors to overcome the negative aspects of the inheritance he passed on to them. The political styles of post-Stalin leaders have differed from the impetuosity of Khrushchev to the cautious approach of Brezhnev, but the substance of the problems they have faced has remained the constant search for a viable institutional reform. The pursuit of improved international understanding and an accommodation with the West (discussed in Chs. 12 and 13) have also been a common thread of policy.

Stalin's successors inherited a system that had remarkable industrial and educational achievements. But it was also a system that had despatched millions of Soviet citizens to labour camps, often under terrible conditions, and had lurched toward a new form of autocracy in which Stalin's policies and intellectual wisdom were beyond challenge. Stalin's failure to realise that a German attack was imminent in June 1941 (see Ch. 12), after all his struggles to build up Soviet defences, provides a spectacular illustration of the political costs of self-deception: the failure of subordinates to speak out, and the insensitivity of an isolated ruling clique to external reality.

The most pressing and immediate concern of Stalin's successors in 1953 was for their own political and physical survival. The previous succession crises, following Lenin's death in 1924, indicated that a

63

Soviet leaders bear the coffin at the funeral of Kalinin in June 1946. From left to right in front: Malenkov, Beria, Molotov, Stalin. (*SCR*)

bruising contest was in prospect. After Stalin's death, the early arrest and subsequent execution of Lavrentii Beria, his close henchman and head of the secret police (the NKVD, forerunner of the KGB), was a key event. Beria, with his voluminous files on every member of the leadership and the organised forces under his command, was a powerful threat to them all. His removal and execution enabled a large measure of political control over the terror apparatus. With Beria gone, his former colleagues could breathe more easily. But significant political questions remained to be answered.

The relatively greater security of members of the new governing elite pointed to the broader issue: How far should mass terror and coercion continue as a form of social control? Terror exerted a numbing effect on initiative and risk taking and on the willingness of officials at all levels of the political system to assume responsibility, with harmful effects on the economy. Moreover, it was not at all clear in 1953 which political institution would hold supreme power. Stalin's rule in his later years was highly personal, based on direct orders to heads of government departments and reinforced by the ultimate threat of the NKVD against recalcitrant officials.

Congresses of the Communist Party and plenary sessions of its key policy-making body, the Central Committee, were few and far between; for example, in violation of Party rules, no congress was convened for a period of 13 years between March 1939 and October 1952. There was no firmly established pattern of *institutional* power in the Soviet Union.

THE KHRUSHCHEV UPHEAVAL (1956–64)

In June 1957, after several years of largely concealed conflict within the top leadership, a decisive political battle took place from which Nikita Khrushchev emerged triumphant. Khrushchev's accession to power provided some important answers to the above questions. As General Secretary of the Communist Party, and one who had cultivated its full-time workers assiduously over several years and used them as a springboard to power, his triumph restored the Party to the institutional pride of place in the political system that it had enjoyed under Lenin. Earlier, at the Twentieth Party Congress in February 1956, Khrushchev had delivered an extraordinary 'secret speech' critical of the political outrages committed under Stalin. This daring manoeuvre was part of the power struggle then approaching its climax, but it also indicated to the Party rank and file that a new era of greater political flexibility was dawning. Past aberrations and mistakes were attributed to Stalin's cult of personality. The speech came like a bolt out of the blue to the delegates, who were utterly unprepared for it; some were unable to hold back tears — whether out of sympathy for the victims and their families or in dismay that deep commitments to the great leader and the steely purpose of their lives were being trailed in the dirt. These revelations marked the end of mass terror. Coercion continued to be used against political and ideological opponents, but less harshly and in a more selective way.

Western observers did not anticipate that these measures, which represented a substantial advance in both political and humanitarian terms, were only a first instalment of what came to be known as 'de-Stalinisation'. The process was by no means complete. Beyond the filling of the institutional power vacuum and the termination of mass terror lay the intractable problem of the economy. It was this problem that finally defeated Khrushchev and most of his successors. The nub of the problem was that the highly centralised form of economic planning that took shape in the USSR in the 1930s, resting on detailed administrative controls over resources and the maximisation of output, became increasingly inappropriate as the economy became larger and more complex. The Moscow-based planning bodies and ministries no longer had a firm grip on what was happening and lacked the capacity to promote rapid technical progress (see Ch. 8). By the mid-1950s, the Soviet Union recognised its enormous technological lag behind the advanced capitalist countries. It became clear that a major reform of the traditional planning mechanism was required (see Chs 3 and 7). A series of political hurdles lay in the path of the reformers, and these proved even more difficult to surmount than the technical difficulties involved in designing the components of a new economic model. Radical economic decentralisation challenged the prevailing view of state socialism in the USSR, which assumed that a supposedly enlightened political elite would determine social goals on behalf of the people and would exercise detailed control over resources to achieve these goals. Economic reform was simultaneously and profoundly *political*. Powerful vested interests were well entrenched and prepared to defend their positions. Reforming political leaders, concerned with maintaining and increasing the momentum of the Soviet economy, could accept this limitation on their aspirations, attempt to circumvent it, or openly contest it. This has been the central problem of Soviet politics since the death of Stalin.

Nikita Khrushchev came from humble origins and, in his youth, had received little formal education. He had no strong claims to intellectual status in a political movement that has always attached importance to the capacity of its leaders to handle Marxist theory. Khrushchev was essentially a practical man and proud of it. But he also possessed an outstanding intuitive grasp of Soviet political problems and, above all, had the courage of his convictions. Khrushchev's notions of economic modernisation did not extend to the introduction of market socialism, but they must have seemed very radical to a generation of managers and officials steeped in the rules of a Stalinist centrally planned economy.

His programme of institutional reform consisted of three major elements. First, the administration of the economy was to be decentralised, with power transferred from the industrial ministries and their obstructive and inward-looking bureaucrats in Moscow to new regional economic councils (*sovnarkhozy*), where it was hoped

66

Nikita Khrushchev (*SCR*)

that economic decisions could be taken in closer congruence with the real world (see Ch. 3). Second, the Communist Party was to be fashioned into an organisation that would play a key role in the development of the economy — a force for practical change rather than a source of empty ideological slogans. This transformation was to be accomplished partly by a substantial turnover in leading personnel, facilitated by a change in the rules governing elections to Party bodies, such as the Central Committee. It also involved a major reorganisation of the entire Party structure, so that in each region responsibility for agriculture and industry was divided between different Party committees. Third, academic experts and specialists were to be drawn into the decision-making process at all levels as a counterweight to conservative official opinion.

Each of these basic policy approaches could be justified on economic grounds. But they also had considerable implications for Khrushchev's own position in relation to possible rivals for power in the leadership. Khrushchev was also personally associated with key 'campaigns' such as the opening up of the Virgin Lands in Kazakhstan to grain cultivation and the attempt to promote the rapid development of the Soviet chemical industry. If these bold or rash initiatives succeeded, Khrushchev stood to gain considerable prestige and power; if they failed, it was likely that his personal position and the strategy of modernisation that he represented would become vulnerable.

Unfortunately for Khrushchev, few of his grandiose domestic policy initiatives lived up to expectations. It is difficult to determine how far their failure was due primarily to obdurate bureaucratic opposition, to lack of time for the measure to take effect, or to their failure to go far enough. Probably all these factors played a part. Khrushchev's position was further weakened by the outcome of his decision to place missiles in Cuba close to the United States, which was a serious miscalculation. In November 1962, his bluff was called by President Kennedy, and this was a great blow to Soviet pride (Ch. 12).

During the early 1960s, opposition to Khrushchev within the Party and government grew. This vividly illustrates the dilemma of a leader bent on reform in the post-Stalin era. A General Secretary of the Party could no longer depend on mass terror to impose his will and secure his authority. He needed tangible success. But this success inevitably depended on overcoming bureaucratic resistance to his policies. The central Party and governmental apparatus was both an impediment to change and an arbiter of its success; accordingly, members affirmed their belief in progress only so long as it did not undermine their own positions. This central paradox in Soviet politics has yet to be resolved.

In October 1964, Khrushchev was removed from power by a vote of the Party Central Committee. This relatively orderly dismissal symbolised, more than any other event, the new political climate and institutional self-confidence that Khrushchev had helped to create. Ironically, this was perhaps his greatest political contribution.

THE EPOCH OF STABILITIES:
BREZHNEV AND AFTER (1964–85)

Khrushchev was replaced by a collective leadership, the most prominent members of which were the new General Secretary of the Party Leonid Brezhnev and the Chairman of the Council of Ministers (Prime Minister) Aleksei Kosygin. It was not long before

Brezhnev, using the Party apparatus as his power base, consolidated his position, much as Khrushchev had done in the 1953–57 period. Although the Soviet leadership has now become more collective in character, Brezhnev nevertheless emerged and became accepted by his peers as a first among equals. His influence (or, more precisely, his failure to exert it) was decisive in setting the tone for the next 18 years.

During the Brezhnev period, the crucial problems of centralised economic management and sluggish innovation became ever clearer and more acute. But Brezhnev's general approach was quite different from that of Khrushchev. Believing that Khrushchev had confronted too many issues at once and taken on too many powerful opponents simultaneously, Brezhnev was prepared to tolerate a more patient and selective approach. In the fundamental political choice between stability and change, his instinct and preference were to favour stability. In trying to discern a pattern in subsequent events, the concept that seems to make most sense is *state corporatism*; this term implies that institutional stability was combined with the controlled expression of key interests within the state. Brezhnev evidently hoped by these means to generate the goodwill among political officials, and the restraint and cooperation among the masses, that would lead to an increase in general welfare. Social-democratic governments in postwar Western Europe, including Labour governments in Britain, operated on a broadly similar basis, but from a much more favourable economic starting point and within an entirely different institutional framework.

State corporatism failed in the Soviet case. Initially, Western specialists were too ready to accept the official Soviet view that Khrushchev had been far too impulsive and prone to 'harebrained schemes', and they gave too much credit to Brezhnev's realism and the possibilities of streamlined socialism. This ignored the fact that both raw enthusiasm and ruffling the feathers of the bureaucracy were objective requirements for change, and failed to appreciate how easily piecemeal reform could degenerate into inertia. Almost immediately after Khrushchev's fall, many of his key institutional reforms were rescinded, including the regional economic councils and the division of the Party into agricultural and industrial wings. The central industrial ministries were restored, but not at first to their former glory. A new major economic reform was introduced by Kosygin in September 1965, giving greater powers to enterprise managers and placing more emphasis on profitability (see Ch. 7). But this reform began to run out of steam after a few years; it effectively petered out after the Prague Spring in 1968 (see Ch. 12), which conservatives denounced as a salutary example of the loss of political control engendered by radical economic reform. With this major policy reverse, the main potential source of economic dynamism of the Brezhnev era disappeared.

The other side of Brezhnev's strategy was to build political bridges to key groups in the bureaucracy and to the masses, and at first this was much more successful. In official circles, life in the USSR became more comfortable and more flexible. There was very little turnover of personnel among leading state and Party officials: 81 per cent of full members of the Party Central Committee elected in 1966 were re-elected in 1971; 89 per cent of the 1971 members were re-elected in 1976. This led to a marked increase in the average age of the Soviet leadership. Some Western specialists and journalists described the Soviet political system during these years as a 'gerontocracy'. (After 1985, the advent of Gorbachev and the ageing of the Reagan administration made the use of such a term inappropriate and imprudent!)

Leonid Brezhnev, Party General Secretary from 1964 to 1982 (*SCR*)

Brezhnev also attempted to build tentative bridges between the Party elite and the masses. Provided that dissent did not become an act of public defiance, individuals were allowed to hold unorthodox opinions and to express them within a confined circle of intimates. The regime turned a blind eye to semilegal economic activities, often conducted under the political protection of prominent officials and even, it later transpired, of Brezhnev himself. Strenuous attempts were made to increase the working class membership of the Party rank and file and to incorporate within the Party the potential leaders of working class opinion. Income differentials, at least in terms of formal salary scales, narrowed considerably during the Brezhnev era to the benefit of industrial workers and, to an even greater extent, the collective farm peasantry. By the early 1970s, highly trained engineers and technicians in industry earned on average only 25 per cent more than manual workers and less than many skilled workers; for scientists working outside industry in specialized institutes and universities, the relativities were even less favourable and declined further as the 1970s progressed. Although scientists and engineers were perhaps less significant in political terms than the bureaucracy or the numerically larger social strata, they were crucial for generating technical progress and economic development.

The political 'deal' on which the Brezhnev era was based did not lead to any appreciable payoff in terms of improved economic performance. In practice, Brezhnev's apparently high-minded trust in cadres masked an extreme reluctance to face the systemic problems bequeathed by Stalin and unresolved by Khrushchev. The rate of economic growth continued to slow down, and by the late 1970s the rate of decline was such that the capacity of the political elite to finance its 'deal' was seriously under threat. A new call for reform began to be heard, especially from intellectuals and technical specialists who had been left out of the 'deal' and resented the privileges and payoffs enjoyed by the political elite, the improved salaries of industrial workers, and the rising incomes obtained by many Soviet citizens from the black economy. When Brezhnev died in November 1982, it is not surprising that members of the Party and government should have had mixed feelings. Obituaries paid eloquent homage to Brezhnev's 'consideration' and 'tact', but there was also impatience with the failings of the economy and a feeling that an important opportunity had been missed. Because these officials were themselves part of the problem, this attitude was

Yuri Andropov (*SCR*)

logically inconsistent and even hypocritical; in private, many felt twinges of guilt and self-disgust.

Brezhnev was replaced as General Secretary of the Communist Party by Yuri Andropov. Andropov was an enigmatic figure, and because he lived for only 15 months after his appointment he remained an enigma. As Chairman of the KGB for most of the period from the late 1960s, Andropov's conservative credentials seemed impeccable. Yet his past and present associations with some leading academic theorists of a more liberal persuasion and his tacit support for Kadar's economic reform in Hungary indicated a more complex character who might favour a mixture of discipline and reform. Andropov did not live long enough to introduce any substantive reform, but he played a crucial role in promoting the debate and preparing the ground for others.

That important initiative was temporarily sidetracked by the promotion of Konstantin Chernenko to the post of General Secretary on Andropov's death in February 1984. Chernenko had spent his early life in Moldavia engaged in ideological work and the latter part of it as the party secretary in charge of Brezhnev's personal office. He had acquired little direct experience in the key policy areas of international affairs or economic management and had no real institutional power base. His appointment was the last ploy of Brezhnev's associates to protect their positions, postponing the day when a younger generation with a more vigorous commitment to reform would take command. That day came sooner than they would have liked. Chernenko survived only 13 months in office and died in March 1985.

The age of Soviet leaders was now an acute embarrassment; the consequences of having avoided a major institutional reform for so long were becoming all too apparent. The economy was in a poor condition. Technological obsolescence and a declining rate of growth had reached the point at which important political objectives were threatened, including parity with the West in newly emerging military technology, satisfaction of a more demanding Soviet consumer, and the provision of an attractive Soviet model of economic and political development to the Third World countries. Soviet power and prestige were at stake. These political consequences of an unreformed economy had been developing over a long period. But the attempts at reform had been bitterly resisted or halfhearted. In the Brezhnev period, some resources had been on hand to provide a cushion against the harsher aspects of change; but this opportunity was wasted. As resources became scarcer, relative to competing demands, economic reform became progressively more painful to implement. By the mid-1980s, economic decline was no longer an abstract prognostication but rather a tangible reality.

GORBACHEV AND PERESTROIKA

Mikhail Gorbachev was elected to the post of General Secretary in March 1985, and it was his fate to take on this daunting challenge. Within a very short time, it became clear that Gorbachev was a new kind of Soviet leader. He was, of course, very much younger and

more highly educated than his immediate predecessors and possessed a spontaneity and talent for public relations that set him apart
from the old guard. But the contrast did not end there. It was the
substance of his policies that took many Western specialists aback,
and arguments raged (and still rage) about how the 'Gorbachev
phenomenon' should be interpreted. Some at first saw his reforms
only as a cosmetic device, designed to appeal to Western public
opinion at a time when arms control negotiations with the United
States and Western Europe were at a critical stage. Others took the
reforms more seriously but believed that they had been introduced
reluctantly and would be withdrawn as soon as they had served the
purpose of improving economic performance and consolidating the
power of the elite. Others accepted that Gorbachev's reforms were
very far-reaching and could lead to irreversible systemic changes but
believed that the forces opposing change were so great that
Gorbachev, like Khrushchev before him, could not possibly
succeed.

We do not yet know conclusively whether these various degrees
of scepticism are justified. At all events, Gorbachev's determined

Mikhail Gorbachev, appointed General Secretary of the Communist Party in March
1985 (*SCR*)

74

attempt to reform the Soviet system fashioned during the Stalin era is entirely logical. *Perestroika* (social reconstruction) is seen by Gorbachev and his advisors as a two-stage process. In the short run, the energies and self-discipline of the labour force (the so-called 'human factor') have to be harnessed so that workers function more productively within the present system of management, using existing equipment. Such expectations have often been entertained by previous Soviet leaders. But the present leaders appreciate that the 'human factor' is a limited resource. In the long run, a sharp acceleration in technical progress is required to catch up with the West, and this, in turn, depends on what are frankly termed 'revolutionary' changes in the political and administrative structure. Initially, the proposed new structures were described in the Soviet literature in a rather coded and oblique way. Gradually, as Gorbachev strengthened his position, the picture became much less opaque. The proposed devolution of power from Moscow-based ministries to industrial enterprises, which will relate to each other substantially (though not exclusively) through market relationships, is discussed in Chapter 7. These proposed measures strike at the heart of the traditional planning system; they go far beyond anything that Khrushchev contemplated.

Will Gorbachev succeed? The parallels with Khrushchev's earlier unsuccessful travails are all too clear. Like Khrushchev, Gorbachev is leading from the front. He is bent on introducing a considerable measure of administrative decentralisation and democratisation and does not shrink from confronting the Soviet bureaucracy directly. When his calls for *perestroika* are not heeded, he resorts, as Khrushchev did, to fiery speeches and appeals for popular support. These parallels are not, on the whole, reassuring. Moreover, a pessimistic reading of the history of modernisation in Russia would suggest that the state has been prone to irrational choice at many phases of its development. It remains to be seen whether the Gorbachev era will mark a decisive departure from this tradition.

On the other hand, there are significant differences from the Khrushchev period as well as from the remoter past. The turnover in Party and government personnel has cut much deeper than it did under Khrushchev, as a new generation takes power. Provided that Gorbachev can operate the levers of promotion effectively, he has a clear opportunity to consolidate his power base. The policy of *glasnost'* (greater openness) also presents him with the possibility of exposing bureaucratic resistance to public scrutiny and mobilising popular opinion on his side. And there is one clinching argument that Khrushchev could not deploy. All varieties of minor tinkering with the traditional system have been tried and found wanting. There does not seem to be any viable alternative to fundamental reform. Gorbachev himself has posed the questions, 'If not us, who, if not now, when?' These are difficult questions for his opponents to answer.

The lack of a coherent platform, however, has not discouraged conservative opponents of *perestroika* from expressing their reservations publicly and, more damagingly, resisting covertly the implementation of major reform measures. In its turn, this bureaucratic obstructionism provoked growing impatience and frustration on the part of Gorbachev and of other leading reformers as they began to sense that the momentum of change was slipping; in particular, the crusade for the hearts and minds of Soviet citizens, on which the fate of the reform ultimately depended, was being lost. By the summer of 1988, the battle lines between reformers and conservatives were drawn – and were perceived – more sharply.

Taking advantage of the General Secretary's absence from Moscow on vacation, his 'number two' in the Kremlin, Egor Ligachev, spelled out in a major policy speech in Gorky the limited political acceptability of market economic relations. He also emphasised the continued relevance of a class-based approach to international affairs. This was a barely concealed attack on two of the major principles of Gorbachev's 'new thinking', which underpinned the reform. At the same time, the chairman of the KGB, Viktor Chebrikov, reiterated his anxieties about the activities of 'informal groups' of Soviet citizens, which had sprung up like mushrooms in the favourable climate of *glasnost'*. In Chebrikov's view, such spontaneous developments took the process of democratisation too far and laid the Soviet polity open to manipulation by hostile external agencies. These confident interventions by senior conservative figures combined with growing public scepticism about the lack of beneficial results of *perestroika* were clear danger signals. On his return from holiday (in a towering rage, it is rumoured) Gorbachev took matters in hand. In a lightning reshuffle of the top leadership Ligachev and Chebrikov were moved sideways (though, in reality, demoted). The veteran former Foreign Minister Andrei Gromyko announced his retirement and, in an emergency forty-five minute session of the Supreme Soviet convened at short notice, Gorbachev was elected President of the USSR, thus combining the office of General Secretary of the Communist Party with that of formal head of state.

At the time of writing, these developments are still very recent and therefore difficult to judge. One recalls the many exaggerated assessments by Western observers of Khrushchev's power after the defeat of his 'Anti-Party Group' opponents in 1957 — only for him to be dismissed in October 1964. Some caution is in order. However, as we have already observed, the pressing economic problems facing Gorbachev are, paradoxically, a political trump card in his favour. There does now seem firm evidence that he has begun to consolidate his power in the top leadership. This is a precondition for *perestroika* but not, of course, *perestroika* itself. It remains to be seen how far the reforming nucleus in the Soviet political leadership, led by Gorbachev, will permit institutionalised opposition and thus pave the way for a change in the relationship between state and society, upon which a fundamental reform depends.

6

Social Classes and
Equality

DAVID LANE

The study of social class in any society is concerned with economic, social, and political inequalities; not only the forms they take in a society and their extent, but also why they exist. Class has to do with the identity of, and the relationships between, groups of people and with the distribution of wealth, power and income among them.

There are two major approaches that seek to explain why inequality of power, status and wealth exists in human society. Some people argue that inequality is 'functionally necessary' to ensure that society operates efficiently and effectively. It is necessary to ensure that the most important positions are conscientiously filled by the best-qualified persons. From this point of view, relationships between social groups are unequal but not combative. Others argue that inequality is a result of the process by which the desirable things in life have become the prerogative of a privileged stratum or class of people who, by a mixture of force, persuasion and manipulation, maintain the status quo in their own interest. According to the view, antagonistic class groups arise that have a potential for social and political conflict.

At the time of the Bolshevik Revolution of October 1917, the Soviet leaders had very clear ideas regarding both the causes of class domination and the future of inequality. For them, inequality was a temporary historical phenomenon, the causes of which were rooted in the ownership of property that gave rise to classes. Inequality was initially a functionally necessary feature of society but, at the same time, was a usurped prerogative of a privileged class. Their approach was derived from the ideas of Karl Marx.

MARXIST THEORY OF CLASS

According to Marx, class is determined by property relations. The owners of property form the kernel of the ruling or exploiting class, whereas those who do not own property are the ruled or exploited class. In modern industrial societies, the bourgeoisie (capitalist class) owns the factories, mines, and other means of production and constitutes the ruling class. It 'exploits' the working class by extracting profit or 'surplus'. The proletariat (working class) is the exploited class, which owns nothing but its ability to work, and sells its labour power to the bourgeoisie. Property ownership gives rights to political power and the means to control the state. For the proletariat, lack of property results in exploitation, in the extraction of the fruits of labour by the bourgeoisie. The labourer has only labour power to sell, 'nothing to lose but his or her chains', and a world to win. In this perspective, proletariat and bourgeoisie have diametrically opposed interests.

Marx argued that the struggle between the proletariat and the bourgeoisie would be resolved by a revolution that would usher in a new epoch of socialism and Communism. A new form of public ownership would be established, and class exploitation would be abolished:

> The condition for the emancipation of the working class is the abolition of all classes. The working class in the course of its development will substitute for the old civic society an association which will exclude classes and their antagonism.

After the victory of the working class, in an intermediate socialist form of society, the means of production would be publicly owned, and people would work according to their ability; owing to the shortage of goods and the need to provide incentives for efficient work, people would be rewarded differently according to the work carried out. Inequality in the sense of distribution of goods and services would thus still remain. In the Communist stage of society, with an abundance of goods and with everyone willing to work for the common interest, individuals would continue to work according to their ability; however, they would now receive according to their need. It was further believed that such a society would make no distinction between mental and manual labour; indeed, there would

A group of Siberian workers (*SCR*)

be no social division of labour, with all persons sharing in all types of work.

What did this theory imply for the Soviet leaders after the October Revolution? First, it is necessary to point out that, even on the Bolsheviks' own testimony, a socialist society was not initially introduced. The Bolsheviks nationalised the land and large-scale industry. But most land was still privately worked; farm implements, as well as many small factories, remained in private ownership. The proletariat had established a political dictatorship known as the *dictatorship of the proletariat*, defending its power against the dispossessed landowners and bourgeoisie. In this important sense, political inequality remained, but society was turned on its head.

At the same time, Lenin and the Bolsheviks had to introduce social institutions appropriate to the new form of society, and this entailed an attack on social inequality. Personal titles, for instance, were abolished, and an attempt was made in the early revolutionary years to introduce mass education through crash programmes. Education was organised on non-authoritarian principles, and polytechnical education was advocated to bridge the gap between mental and manual labour (see Ch. 10). An attempt was made to reduce wage differentials, and party members were not entitled to more than a fixed, 'party maximum' wage.

The year 1931 was a turning point. Stalin pointed out to the Soviet public that workers in the socialist stage of society were expected to 'give according to their ability and to receive according to their work', not according to need. Until this time, unequal rewards had generally been regarded as something that had to be tolerated as a temporary necessity, but that should be greatly reduced, even in the socialist stage of society. However, Stalin stressed in an interview with Emil Ludwig, the German writer, that 'the kind of socialism under which everybody would get the same pay, an equal quantity of meat and an equal quantity of bread, would wear the same clothes and receive the same goods in the same quantities, such a socialism is unknown to Marxism'. He added, 'Only people who are unacquainted with Marxism can have the primitive notion that the Russian Bolsheviks want to pool all wealth and share it out equally'; this was the idea of Communism held by primitive 'Communists' at the time of Cromwell and the French Revolution.

Nevertheless, although there were *income differentials* in the new Soviet state, from 1936 it was denied that there were any antagonistic classes in a Marxist sense. In theory, there was *distributional* inequality but not *political* inequality. The Soviet view of the Soviet Union was one of class harmony, not of class struggle. There were still two major classes, however, the working class and the collective farm peasantry. The collective farmers constituted a class because they collectively still owned their tools (not the land) and their products as a co-operative unit, and were not directly employed by the socialist state. A further stratum of professional, technical and clerical personnel, usually referred to as the intelligentsia, was seen as constituting a distinct major social group, but it was not a class because it had no special relationship to the ownership of the means of production. In the Soviet view, the interests of these three groups did not conflict in any fundamental ways. A Soviet textbook describes the situation in the Soviet Union as follows: 'Since they jointly own social property, and jointly participate in the social production process, all people are equal and their relations are based on principles of comradely co-operation and mutual assistance'.

81

Meal-time in the field for the collective farm workers in the Kiev region (*SCR*)

Thus there were no property-owning classes and, therefore, no ruling class and no exploited class; consequently, social harmony prevailed.

These conclusions are insufficient to describe social relations in the USSR. It is difficult, in terms of this theory, to explain why it was necessary to enforce a one-party system in which the party was the leader of the working class, or indeed to have a state at all. Soviet writers turned for justification to the international political order that constituted a threat to the security of the USSR and justified the continuation of a state apparatus. In addition to political inequality, there are major distributional inequalities; in life-style, in income and in status between groups of individuals in the contemporary Soviet Union.

KINDS AND EXTENT OF INEQUALITY

In the Soviet view of things, as we have seen, there are three non-antagonistic social groups: in 1985, the collective farmers made up approximately 9.6 per cent of the working population; the

82

Returning home from the pastures (*SCR*)

manual working class, 62.7 per cent; and the intelligentsia and other white-collar workers, 27.7 per cent.

Collective farmers have a co-operative form of production. They collectively own the seeds, produce and machinery of the farms. A considerable part of their income is derived from agricultural production on their personal plots, the produce of which they are free to sell on the market. Cultural and educational standards are much lower than in the towns. There are major differences in consumption patterns and social services. Political participation in the Communist Party and in the organs of government is lower than for the other two social groups. With the development of the economy, however, a gradual narrowing of these differences has been taking place.

The main characteristic of the other two groups is the place they occupy in the division of labour. The intelligentsia are 'workers by brain' and include some white-collar workers in clerical and executive jobs, as well as people in administrative, directive, and creative roles. The top subgroups of this stratum have higher salaries and are better educated; a high proportion of them are Party members.

Manual workers are divided into two subgroups, the skilled and unskilled. This class as a whole is occupied in physical work. On average, but with important exceptions, workers receive lower wages than do the intelligentsia. They have, at best, a secondary education; their cultural standards are lower than those of the intelligentsia, but higher than those of the peasantry. They are well represented in the Party, but there are relatively fewer of them than the intelligentsia.

If we consider three major aspects of distributional inequality — the pattern of income, the social status of occupations, and access to education — it becomes clear that a significant hierarchy exists in the contemporary USSR.

First, consider the pattern of income. It is certainly true that since the mid-1950s wage differentials have narrowed and there has been an improvement in the lowest rate. The minimum official wage (80 rubles per month) is 42 per cent of the average wage (190.1 rubles in 1985). Data are available for different categories of employees in industry. These show that over the past 25 years manual workers have improved their position compared to engineers and technicians, whereas clerical workers have fallen badly behind. Thus, in 1960, engineering and technical employees received average salaries 48 per cent higher than manual workers; in 1985, this advantage had fallen to only 10 per cent. Clerical workers received 18 per cent less than manual workers in 1960 and as much as 22 per cent less in 1985. But a wide range of incomes still remains.

Our knowledge of differentials is handicapped by the insufficiencies of Soviet statistical reporting. In 1985, as compared with the average wage of 190 rubles a month, research professors in the Academy of Sciences received, on average, more than 1200 rubles a month. Government ministers received, as a minimum, more than 1700 rubles a month. Factory managers earned between 500 and 1500 rubles; a leading composer might earn as much as 8000 rubles. These figures may underestimate the real differences because some forms of income are acquired through privilege or taken in kind. Many Western commentators have suggested that the differential is much higher than suggested by these figures. Special advantages for the elite include special shops, restaurants, holiday facilities, and such perks as the availability of cars. The reforms of Gorbachev seek to abolish such 'unearned' and unjust incomes. The largest differential reported in Western emigre sources is a ratio of 300:1 between the highest income and the lowest income, and a ratio of 100:1 between the highest and average incomes. Even if these ratios are overstated, there can be no doubt that a vast gap exists between the life-styles of the elite and the average worker. Even so, it is much lower than in the United States where it is estimated that the ratio between the highest and lowest incomes is 11000:1 and the ratio between the highest and average incomes is 7000:1. Many commentators would emphasize the 'greyness' and relative distributional uniformity of the USSR compared to that in the West. Indeed one of the consequences of the reforms introduced in the late 1980s is an increase in income differentials.

How do these income scales influence the status — the honour or the deference — individuals enjoy in society? Do high incomes give people honour? Is there a hierarchy status? Very few empirical data are available on these points. There does seem to be a hierarchy of status closely connected to occupation. At the top are the creative professional people, such as scientists, astronauts, doctors and engineers; at the bottom are manual, unskilled workers. Research on the esteem of jobs in different societies reveals that occupations in the Soviet Union, the United States, Germany, and to a lesser extent, Great Britain are given very similar rankings. Preferences of school leavers give quite a good indication of the desirability of certain jobs. In a list of eighty occupations, school children ranked at the top physicist, engineer, medical scientist, and engineer/geologist. At the bottom, they ranked household maintenance worker, printing press operator, agricultural worker, and painter. Other studies show that physicians have high esteem, whereas clerical workers and shop sales personnel have low evaluations. Women tend to be clustered in many of the jobs in low-paid industries and have lower skill ratings than do men. They earn on average about 30 to 40 per cent less than do men. This ratio is similar to that in Britain, though it must be borne in mind that a much higher proportion of women in the USSR are in paid employment.

Educational opportunity is the main avenue for social advancement in the Soviet Union. Who has access to education in the Soviet Union? Are any specific groups excluded? In the West, middle and

85

upper occupational groups seem to have a much greater chance for a higher education than do the workers. Is this also true in the Soviet Union? The short answer is that there are similarities.

Table 1   *Aspirations of Soviet school leavers (a) and social background of students attending various higher educational institutions (b)*

a.

Groups to which parents belong	Proportion of school leavers wishing to:			Proportion of school leavers subsequently actually engaged in:		
	Work %	Work with study %	Study %	Work %	Work with study %	Study %
urban intelligentsia	2	5	93	15	3	82
workers in industry and building	11	6	83	36	3	61
agricultural workers	10	14	76	90	—	10
Per cent of total	7	10	83	37	2	61

b.

	Manual %	Non-manual %	Peasants %	Total %
USSR (all students)	43	39	18	100
Kazakhstan	49	41	10	100
USSR population	57	22	21	100

Table 1 indicates the aspirations of children and also the ways in which these aspirations are actually fulfilled after children leave school. As shown, 93 per cent of school leavers with a non-manual background wished to continue to study after the compulsory school-leaving age, and 82 per cent subsequently did continue to study. Of agricultural workers, 76 per cent wanted to continue to study but only 10 per cent actually did so. One can conclude from these figures that there is an enormous and widespread demand for further education in the USSR. And there is differential access to education after the compulsory school-leaving age. Other studies show the occupational background of students in different areas of the USSR. Part b of Table 1 shows that children of people in non-manual occupations have a much higher chance of access to higher educational institutions than their share in the population

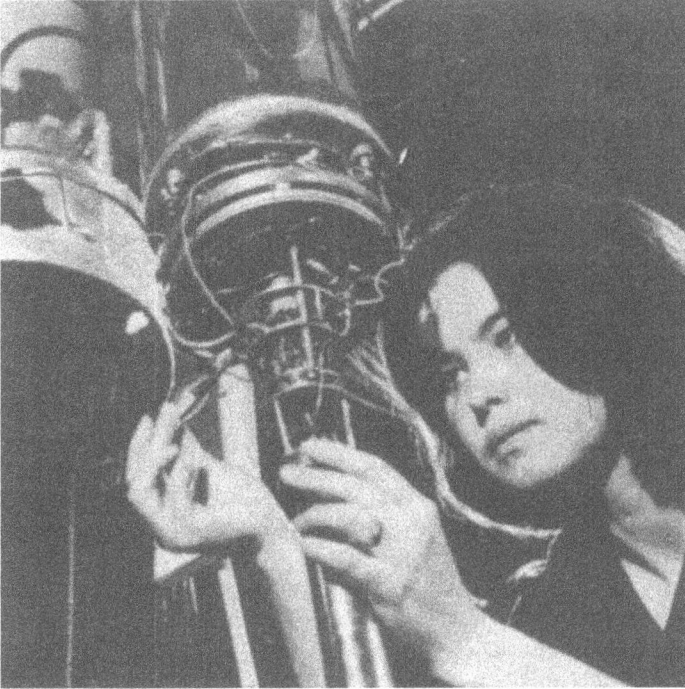

A research associate of the Joint Nuclear Research Institute (*SCR*)

would warrant. Nevertheless, one should not minimise the opportunities available to children in the Soviet Union. As shown in Table 1a, children of manual workers do continue at institutions of higher education, and more than 60 per cent of children of workers in industry and building continued their schooling.

Is the system becoming more hereditary? The brief answer is that, over time, there has been greater internal recruitment from within given social groups. In the past, there certainly has been a very great inflow to higher status positions as a consequence of the very high rate of economic development. As the rate of economic development falls off, it seems that the extent of upward mobility is lessening and that the occupational structure has become somewhat more hereditary. It should be emphasised, however, that there is still very considerable upward mobility and that opportunities are widely available for children of manual workers and of peasants.

THE PERSISTENCE OF SOCIAL STRATIFICATION

The existence of stratification and social inequality in the contemporary Soviet Union is clearly established in terms of income, status and educational opportunity. Each of these criteria cuts across the conventional Soviet division of the population into workers, peasants and intelligentsia. Within the intelligentsia, in particular, there is a very wide dispersion of income, status and educational opportunity — from the elite of scientists, writers and administrators living in Moscow or Leningrad at one extreme, to the poorly paid minor technicians and clerical workers in small provincial towns, at the other.

How can the persistence of inequality be explained? Part of the answer lies in what might be called 'political position'. Various groups are located in strategic positions in the administrative state system and are able to control resources to their own advantage. Under Gorbachev a serious attempt is being made to lessen such administrative control. Other 'elitist' groups in the economy, in culture, in the army, and in the administration are able to exert pressure to secure their own privilege. But the manual working class in industry has improved its position; this is related to the leaders' concern with maintaining social solidarity. Moreover, full employment and a labour shortage give workers a good bargaining position with respect to management.

Another, and perhaps more fundamental, factor is the division of labour between different occupations. Occupational status differentiates various groups of individuals. The directing, intellectual and cultural occupations appear to be more universally desired by members of society. These jobs are more interesting, they influence one's way of life and leisure interests, and they affect educational selection and the choice of a spouse. People compete for these positions. Occupation gives status, and the status hierarchy is, to some extent, independent of power and income. Exposure to different kinds of education in itself leads to a differentiated life-style and to aspirations to a certain way of life. Even if there were a very narrow income differential, there would still be a status hierarchy; at least Soviet experience would seem to suggest this.

On the supposition that equality is a major goal for a society desiring to become communist, how can it be furthered? Four major conditions seem to be necessary.

First, greater material wealth is necessary. A higher level of production would reduce the material shortages that at present exist in the Soviet Union. It should not be forgotten that there are insufficient resources at present to provide adequate living space for everyone who wants it. The Soviet Union is still at a lower level of development than are the advanced capitalist countries of the West.

Second, with the development of the productive forces to a much higher level than at present, the division of labour could be reduced, and manual and non-manual occupations could be merged. This stage is still a long way off. But one cannot begin to think of abolishing distinctions between manual and non-manual work when a large proportion of the work force is engaged in manual labour.

Third, greater popular participation in public affairs is required. There are significant distinctions in the Soviet Union between those who give orders and those who carry them out. This has led some Western critics to argue that the USSR has a ruling class made up of those who control the state-owned means of production. This is an issue that cannot be pursued here. It should be noted, however, that this is not the same kind of exploiting class as defined by Marx, as there is no longer the extraction of profit or surplus by a class. If there is a ruling class, it is a dominant political class. It is certainly the case that a socialist society cannot be achieved without greater levels of real mass participation than are known today. This will have implications for Party control, and the centralised nature of power will need to be changed. Under Gorbachev there is a significant move away from the kinds of central control which were instituted under Stalin.

Finally, a weaker form of family structure is necessary to achieve greater equality; this, in turn, would involve greater communal care of children. A more important role played by communal institutions would reduce the ability of families higher in the status hierarchy to pass on their advantages to their offspring, and result in greater opportunities for the children in lower social strata. Present trends, however, show little evidence of this happening.

7

The Economic System

PHILIP HANSON

The Soviet economy is the largest centrally administered production system in the world. (China has a much larger population than the USSR but a smaller total output of goods and services.) The official Soviet description of the economy calls it a 'planned, socialist economy'. The words *planned* and *socialist* could mean many things. So far as the Soviet economy is concerned, planned means that the output of every farm, factory, construction organisation — even, in principle, the research 'output' of scientists — is determined by instructions from above that are part of a single, national plan. Socialist means that private enterprise, with a few limited exceptions, is outlawed; all able-bodied citizens of working age, except students and mothers of small children, work in a state or cooperative enterprise or in some other state organisation where, of course, all are working to fulfil the national plan. A small amount of officially approved self-employment also exists, but it is restricted to students, invalids and pensioners, and able-bodied people of working age who work for themselves part-time.

These operational definitions of planned and socialist have been in effect in Soviet state policy from the late 1920s to the present. Anyone who has worked or studied in a large organisation knows, of course, that what actually happens is not always what the top management says is happening. The reality of Soviet economic practice can and does deviate from the official description of that reality, sometimes in surprising ways. And the detailed official arrangements that operate in different parts of the production system are necessarily diverse and complicated. Nonetheless, the basic principles, state ownership and detailed state control of production, are fundamental to the way the Soviet system works. Let us first consider ownership, which is less complicated, and then control.

The giant rolling mill of the Novolipetsk factory (*SCR*)

OWNERSHIP

Almost all productive resources, that is land, mineral reserves and other natural resources, production equipment, factory and farm buildings, railway lines, research laboratories, and so on, are owned by the state. By far the greater part of production is carried out by state enterprises. There are two main exceptions. First, there are the collective farms or *kolkhozy*, which, in the strict legal sense, are producer cooperatives rather than state enterprises. In 1985, they were responsible for about 30 per cent of all farmland. The land itself is all state-owned, but the collective farms are the legal owners of their buildings, equipment and livestock. They are, however, very much under state control. In practical terms, the collective farms can be treated as part of the state sector. (Collective farms are discussed further in Ch. 9.)

The second main exception is what the Soviets call 'personal economic activity'. In official speeches and writings, they make a point of not calling it the private sector. The reason is that in Soviet official doctrine private enterprise is capitalist; capitalism entails the exploitation of workers by the non-working, property-owning class, and such exploitation cannot, by definition, occur in the Soviet Union. This is not just a matter of words. Soviet legislation does not allow anyone who is working for himself (personal economic activity) to employ anybody else, though family members may work together in this sector. Thus, there is some scope for private self-employment but not, at any rate not legally, for private employment. Moreover, the private sector is limited in two other ways. First, able-bodied adults of working age have an obligation to work (unemployment for more than a short period of time is a punishable offence), and until now at least (early 1988), they have had to work for the state; therefore, self-employment, except for pensioners and invalids, is allowed only as a spare-time activity. Second, part-time self-employment is limited in practice by the central system of control over property and materials. For a would-be café owner to rent premises or a would-be small builder to obtain bricks and timber, legally at any rate, has traditionally been almost impossible.

Nonetheless, the personal or private sector is important for the everyday material welfare of the population. More than a quarter of food production comes from the personal smallholdings (*very* small holdings of generally less than an acre) of collective farm households and other citizens. Most of this food is consumed by the families who produce it, but a significant amount is traded in rural areas and also sold on the *kolkhoz* (collective-farm) markets in the cities. These markets, incidentally, like markets anywhere, are fascinating for the foreign tourist to visit. In addition, there is a considerable amount of spare-time private economic activity: repair work, medicine, tutoring, and all kinds of wheeling and dealing in tapes, books, jeans, video-cassettes, and other items in short supply.

The dividing line between what is and is not legal in private economic activity has never been clearly drawn. The present leadership, in its efforts to revitalise the Soviet economy, is seeking to encourage personal economic activity and a new type of small producer cooperative in the service sector and in some other fields. A new law introduced in late 1986 is intended to clarify the legal position, to demonstrate the state's backing for certain kinds of private activity, and, at the same time, to regulate and tax private enterprise. There has, so far, been no relaxation of the rule that the self-employed may not employ other people, despite the fact that private firms with small numbers of employees are allowed in most East European countries (e.g. staffs of up to ten in East Germany). Nor has there yet been any clear departure from the rule about such activity being only spare-time.

Nobody knows just how large the Soviet private sector really is, just as nobody knows reliably the size of the so-called 'black economy' in Western countries. It is clear, however, that the overwhelming bulk of production is carried out in the state production establishment. How this state production system is controlled by the central authorities is the most remarkable feature of the Soviet economy. This detailed central control of production is one of the things that makes living and working in the USSR very different from living and working in a Western country.

A law on cooperatives, passed in 1988, opens up possibilities for a major expansion of cooperative production, outside direct state control, in all sections of the economy. So far, however, this new cooperative sector is small.

CENTRAL PLANNING

At the end of 1985, there were 49000 state and collective farms in the Soviet Union, together with 46000 state industrial enterprises, 42000 construction organisations, and 710000 retail shops and stalls; a considerable number of other management units were involved in transport, research, services, and the many other activities that make up a modern economy. Every one of those units is given an annual production plan, containing targets which it is legally obliged to make every effort to fulfil. (In some cases, of course, the plan concerns sales, e.g. for shops, or the movement of goods, e.g. for transport organisations, but these are all part of the production process in a broad sense.)

What is produced according to the plan is also distributed and used according to the plan. An important exception is the final sale of consumer goods to the population, which depends on what people choose to buy out of what is made available to them. Each factory is told (at least in broad terms) what materials are being allocated for it to use and where they are to come from. Correspondingly, its output is allocated by the planners to other factories or to the state distribution system. This is on the basis of 'material balances', balances of the production and use of different items, worked out by the planners. In fulfilling its production plan and disposing of its output, the state farm or factory has to work with a set of prices controlled by the central planners, has to abide by centrally decreed pay scales for different jobs, and has to operate within various planned limits on its spending (for example, on its wage bill).

In a Western capitalist economy, most production is not centrally controlled. It is true that the modern state intervenes heavily in the economy. In Britain at present, the public sector employs about a quarter of the working population, and most of what goes on in the public sector could be described as centrally planned. Even so, by far the greater part of the nation's supply of consumer goods and services, and of the machinery and know-how to produce them, is privately produced (or imported from foreign private producers). So far as that predominant part of national output is concerned, the decisions about what is produced, and in what quantities, are not taken by any central authority. No detailed information about planned output is provided by the private sector to the government, and no national plans exist to match the total supply to the total use of, say, numerically controlled machine tools, let alone to tell each machine-tool producer how many machines to produce, who receives the finished products, and who supplies the necessary materials and equipment. These decisions reached by individual firms in a Western economy through their dealings with one another are arrived at in the USSR by means of a detailed central plan.

That means that all the hundreds of thousands of basic management units in the economy receive yearly plan instructions regarding their production. The immensity of this planning task is hard to grasp. It is not just that each enterprise is told to produce X million rubles' worth of whatever it is able to produce. Each enterprise has specific instructions about specific products. This is unavoidable in detailed central planning of this kind.

For example, factories that are producing tractors require certain quantities of sheet steel of specific grades, and the supply of that steel is itself allocated by the central plan. Therefore, the planners have to fix the amount to be produced and who is to produce it so that it can

Factory college — the design of the car engine is explained to students. (*SCR*)

be allocated to the planned users. For the 1987 plan, for example, the 60 or so enterprises that come under the Ministry of Heavy Engineering each received obligatory targets for total sales, labour productivity, costs, and the main products each had to produce, plus a further 60 semi-obligatory 'indicators' on which they were given assignments and on which they had to report progress: 40 of these indicators related to the introduction of new technology, 9 to environmental protection, 7 to required organisational changes, and so on. Moreover, the list of main products to be produced came to 358. Obviously, only some of these are produced by any particular enterprise, but it is clear that each enterprise could easily be receiving a plan containing a hundred or more indicators to be fulfilled and reported on. A roughly similar targeting process took place in some 60 branch ministries, between them covering the whole economy. The central planners are supposed to ensure that all these millions of targets fit together into a national plan for total production that is feasible, internally consistent, and, if possible, efficient in accomplishing the broad, overall aims of the top policymakers.

It is obvious that this gigantic exercise in detailed central planning is impossible, given the numbers of people, places, products, and production units involved. But it works. That is to say, the economy does not break down, production almost always increases from year to year, and there is full employment. One reason why it works is that the central planners do not try directly to calculate all the many millions of specific instructions to specific production units. Instead, they work out broad aggregate totals for main categories of production (and for some particular products that are deemed especially important) and assign to the branch ministries (such as the ministries for the steel and chemical industries) the responsibility for working out the detailed instructions to particular production units. These detailed instructions are supposed to fit into the broad totals set by the central planners.

The central planners consist of the staffs of the State Planning Committee (Gosplan), the State Material–Technical Supply Committee (Gossnab), the State Committee for Prices, the State Committee for Science and Technology, and other 'functional' bodies reporting to the Council of Ministers, that is organisations that deal with particular aspects of the economy as a whole rather than with particular branches of the economy. Gosplan is perhaps the most central of all these central planning bodies. It has overall responsibility for the national plan; its status is reflected in the fact that its chairman is a first deputy prime minister and a candidate member of the Politburo. The central planners work out 'material balances' (see the discussion on central planning) for about 18 000 products. In other words, they work out, by broad organisational categories, who is to produce how much of each of these items and who is to receive how much of each item. These material balances, in turn, are broken down into specific supply allocations for specific production units, both as producers and as users.

PROBLEMS OF CENTRALISED ADMINISTRATION

This system works, but it does not work well. All known economies have their problems, of course, and these problems are not just the result of the economic system. Some capitalist economies, at any given time, function better than others, and the same can be said about socialist economies. Bad policies, unfavourable developments on world markets, internal social conflicts inherited from past national propensities to idleness and sloppy work (as a result of past history) — all these can affect any nation's economic performance as it is usually measured. (Incidentally, the indulging of a desire to be idle is a contribution to human happiness and ought to be allowed for when measuring national output; alas, nobody knows how to measure it.) Nevertheless, different economic systems undoubtedly generate different patterns of economic behaviour. The strengths and weaknesses in economic performance are different for each economic system. Both Western capitalism and Soviet socialism produce problems. It is important in understanding the Soviet Union today to grasp that its economic system generates problems quite unlike those we are familiar with in the West, and that these systemic problems have come to preoccupy the Soviet political leadership.

Hence all the talk about economic reform. Gorbachev has spoken repeatedly of the need for a 'radical restructuring' of the system of economic planning and management. In a speech in April 1986, he said: 'Can the economy really be run by trillions of calculations from Moscow? That's absurd, comrades! And that is where the greatest mistake lies, in the fact that until very recently we have tried to run everything from Moscow'. The present Soviet leader evidently wants to change the economic system in more than a minor way, and it is important to understand why.

The present economic system rests on detailed instructions to all production units. Instructions from above play a part in all economic systems, but in the West such instructions about production are issued inside each of a great many different organisations, some large and some small. The Soviet system is run as a single, giant hierarchy. Instead of market dealings between large numbers of mini-hierarchies, there is an overwhelming predominance of vertical relationships. This creates both an information system and a pattern of human motivation that differ from the information and motivation arrangements of a Western economy.

Consider the example of one engineering factory under the Ministry of Heavy Engineering. Each year it receives, as we have seen, a large number of targets from its ministry. The ministry, in turn, is given a large number of targets by the central planners. The

97

details vary from industry to industry, but the general pattern is the same. The factory, when it is a separate management unit in its own right, stands to receive bonuses for management staff and, to a smaller extent, for all other staff, in accordance with its performance in fulfilling these targets. The enormous scale of the central planning exercise makes it virtually certain that not all these targets will be consistent with one another. For instance, it may be possible to fulfil the total output target but impossible to fulfil simultaneously all the detailed targets for the output of particular products. The factory manager is therefore obliged to make some choices among the various targets. In doing so, the manager may sacrifice a particular output instruction that should be fulfilled if some other enterprise's supply of machinery is to be forthcoming.

More importantly, the manager has every incentive to secure a high allocation of materials and equipment, given the output targets, or, to put it the other way round, to obtain a low production plan target, given the allocation of materials and equipment. What counts

Socialist competition — a group of workers receives a banner acknowledging their success in production — a well-practised form of incentive in Soviet industry. (*SCR*)

is not what the purchasers of the equipment want, but what the superior authorities tell the manager to do.

The authorities cannot, however, know as much as the manager does about what the plant can produce. Therefore, his object is to get an easy plan, regardless of what the purchasers want provided. This attempt may not succeed, but the superior authorities depend for information, to some extent, on the manager, who tries to manoeuvre them into agreeing to an easy plan.

The incentive system has other effects that are not obvious at first sight. The factory manager does not know what the target for next year will be, but it is generally influenced by the current year's results. If the target is overfulfilled this year, there is an additional bonus, but the target for future years goes up. These two considerations must be weighed against one another. It seems, generally, that Soviet factories try to obtain the lowest possible targets and overfulfil them narrowly. For similar reasons, they usually have very little interest in lowering production costs by economising on labour and materials or by introducing new, cost-cutting technology. The more inputs the better, as far as factory managers are concerned, as retooling to introduce new technology into the factory will usually interfere with meeting the year's main targets. It usually also does nothing to help future bonuses. This is because any increase that results in greater productive capacity or a reduction in materials or labour requirements will either be kept secret from the higher authorities or, if revealed, will result in more demanding targets being set for the enterprise.

Soviet enterprises generally behave in this way in most lines of production. This is well known throughout Soviet industry and not seriously disputed in Soviet writings about the economy. Figure 9, taken from a Soviet management journal, illustrates this. Managers and senior officials often win medals for results that look good on paper but that, as everyone close to the action knows, do not reflect reality. The journal *EKO* suggested some more appropriate medals that would reflect reality.

Some examples can illustrate the weaknesses of the Soviet system. In the early 1980s, Soviet factories began to produce a new generation of tractors. These tractors had more powerful engines than did earlier models and were, in several other respects, an improvement. But no ploughs, harrows, trailers or other attachments were made to fit them, so they brought no benefit to the

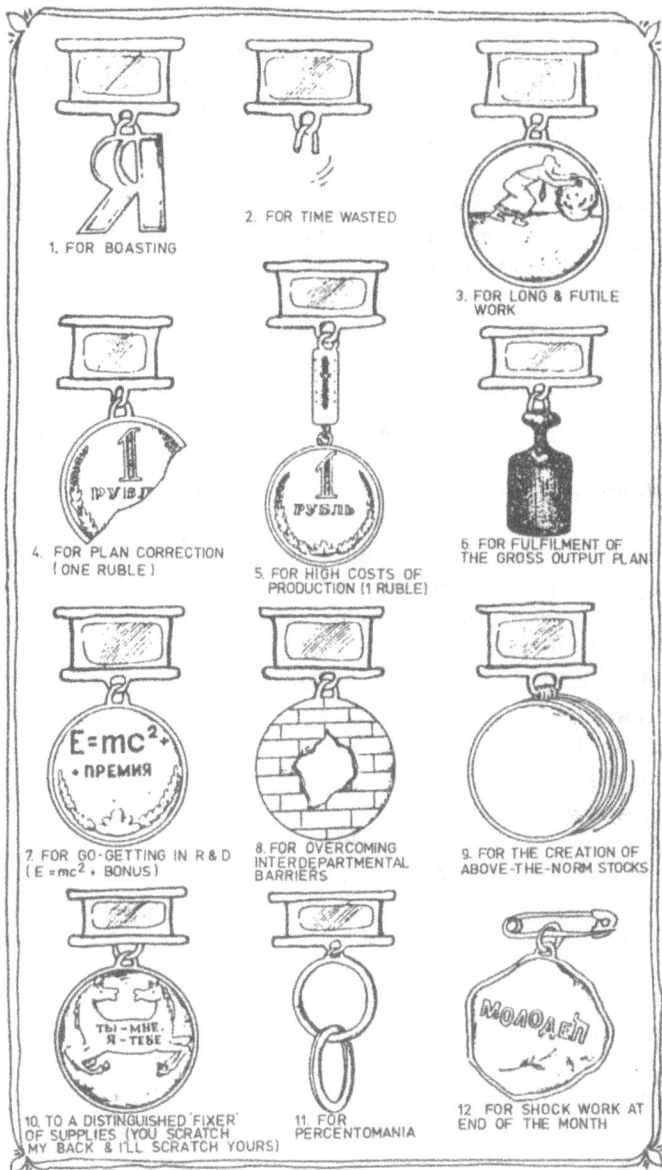

Figure 9 *The Soviet journal EKO wryly suggests some new medals, to be awarded for some of the more dubious 'achievements' of industrial management and officials*

100

farms, where tractors have to be hooked up to various kinds of machinery. As long as the factories were meeting their production targets for the number and capacity of tractors, however, they were not concerned; their customers' requirements were not important.

Even well-intentioned campaigns to counter defects of the system often produce damaging results because of the predominance of plan targets over customer needs. It was discovered a few years ago that scrap metal delivered to scrapyards for recycling contained large quantities of unused, new engineering components. Because of past shortages of spare parts, factories had been given special bonuses for producing spare parts: the more spare parts, the larger the bonus. At the same time, to encourage the recycling of scrap metal, there were bonuses for delivering scrap metal. By making more components than were needed and sending them straight to the scrapyard, factories were collecting both bonuses. As long as the higher authorities were unaware of what was going on, there was nothing to deter the factory managers from doing this. Nothing in the system motivated them to avoid unnecessary production.

The central authorities manage to enforce more efficient behaviour in a few industries that have top-priority status and that are especially closely supervised; in practice, this means mainly military production. This is a substantial part of Soviet output — defence spending is some 15 to 17 per cent of national income, or more than twice as large a share as in the United States — but it is, nonetheless, only a narrow sector of the economy.

These weaknesses have a fundamental effect on Soviet life. The living standard of ordinary Soviet citizens has, on the whole, improved over time (though there was a halt to this progress for a time in the early 1980s), but it remains low by West European standards. It is true that the system also generates full employment because demand for all inputs into production, including labour, tends to be inflated. It is also true that the system provides some growth from year to year. What has made the Soviet leadership consider radical changes in the economic system is that this growth has become slower and slower. The prospect of relative, perhaps even absolute, economic decline loomed before the Soviet economy in the mid-1980s and was coupled with a continued technological lag behind the West (see Ch. 8).

Until the early 1970s, the Soviet Union was catching up with the United States in total production. This was important because the

Living standards have improved over time but remain low by West European standards.

United States is Moscow's rival military superpower and the flagship of the capitalist world — not the fastest-growing capitalist economy, but politically by far the most important and, on the whole, the most technologically advanced. In the long run, Soviet military power rests, as it does in any modern state, on economic power. The international prestige of the Soviet system also seemed to rest on its ability to show that the major socialist economy, though more backward than the major capitalist economy, was catching up with its rival. But, since the mid-1970s, even Soviet estimates have shown Soviet national income stuck at two-thirds of the U.S. level. United States' estimates (using a rather different definition of national income) show Soviet national income now at about half that of the United States, and tending to fall relative to that level in recent years.

The weaknesses of the system are not the only reasons for the Soviet economic slowdown. There are several others that may be equally important, including the reduced rate of growth of the population and labour force and the depletion of the more easily exploited natural resources in the western part of the country. It should also be noted that, with basically the same centralised system that it has now, the Soviet economy grew quickly up to about 1960.

Nonetheless, it is clear that the traditional, highly centralised system is not good for technological innovation in a mature industrial economy and that technological progress must, in future, be relied upon as the main source of long-term economic growth.

The Gorbachev leadership has, therefore, embarked on a programme of serious economic reform. It has five main elements. Small-scale private and cooperative production are to be expanded (the latter will possibly be unplanned and really a polite form of private enterprise). Most obligatory targets for state enterprises are to be abolished and replaced by a mixture of broad plan guidelines, market relations (buying and selling between state enterprises), and something like 'commercial orders' from the state. Many prices are to be set by negotiation between buyers and sellers. Most (but not all) centralised allocation of materials to producers is to be abolished. State enterprises are to be required to finance their operating costs and most of their investment from their sales revenue and to pay a kind of profits tax to the state budget.

Mr Gorbachev meets the workers in a new-style walkabout. (*SCR*)

By and large, these changes exist at present (1988) only on paper. They are supposed to be introduced by the end of 1990 so that the reformed system would be operational by the start of the Thirteenth Five-Year Plan on 1 January 1991. Whether these changes can be successfully introduced in practice is uncertain. Both bureaucratic resistance and the doubts and scepticism of a large part of the labour force have to be overcome.

Even if this 'market socialist' reform is carried out in practice, it will probably not bring the kind of competition that is normal in capitalist economies, where firms that fail to control costs or keep up with technological change are driven out of business or taken over by other firms, with accompanying job losses. Yet, it probably takes that sort of competition to force producers to be efficient and to adopt the latest technology. If the reforms are implemented, therefore, they still may not bring high quality production and rapid productivity growth to the USSR. And it is productivity growth, even if it causes insecurity in many people's working lives, that raises the average level of material prosperity in a country.

There is, therefore, no certainty that any economic reform is feasible that would be both politically acceptable to the Party leadership and capable of transforming Soviet economic performance. Soviet conservatives can rightly argue that the present system has a considerable rugged stability, even if it lacks dynamism. Under Gorbachev's leadership, however, the search for a more dynamic economic system is underway.

8

Science and Technology

JULIAN COOPER

Soon after his election as General Secretary of the Soviet Communist Party, Mikhail Gorbachev posed the central issue facing the country in stark terms. Speaking at a plenary session of the party's Central Committee in April 1985, he briefly reviewed the difficulties of the late Brezhnev years and then went on:

> The country's historic destiny and the position of socialism in the present-day world depend, in large measure, on how we . . . act further. By making wide-scale use of the achievements of the scientific and technological revolution and by bringing the forms of socialist economic management into line with modern conditions and requirements, we must achieve a substantial acceleration of social and economic progress. There is simply no other way.

The present Soviet leaders clearly perceive that science and technology have a crucial role to play in the revitalisation of Soviet socialism. But the present position is far from satisfactory. As Gorbachev has acknowledged, peaks of technological modernity coexist with plains of backwardness:

> Our rockets can find Halley's comet and fly to Venus with amazing accuracy, but side-by-side with these scientific triumphs is an obvious lack of efficiency in using scientific achievements for economic needs, and many Soviet household appliances are of poor quality.

What accounts for this situation? How can Gorbachev raise the lowlands of Soviet technology to the heights of the foremost Western countries? Will he succeed?

In the early years of the Soviet regime, it was taken for granted that socialism, with its social ownership and central planning, would enable a rate of scientific and technical progress inconceivable under capitalism. The rapid industrialisation of the 1930s lent support to this optimism: technology in the Soviet Union surged forward; the capitalist world was wracked by economic crisis. Since those early days, experience has provided some sobering lessons: capitalism has demonstrated a long-term capability for technological innovation unthinkable to Marxists of an earlier generation; socialism has not, in practice, demonstrated an inherent superiority in its ability to secure the rapid advancement of science and technology to benefit society as a whole.

TECHNOLOGY AND THE ECONOMIC PYRAMID

To a considerable extent, the problems now facing the Soviet leadership have their origins in the strategy and methods of economic development adopted during that dramatic prewar industrialisation drive and maintained with relatively minor changes into the 1980s. This was 'extensive' development: it was achieved by drawing in large quantities of readily available, low-cost resources. High-quality resources of all kinds, including technical skills, were in extremely short supply and were concentrated in sectors considered essential for the survival of the Soviet state and for the creation of a capacity for independent development. Priority activities included military production, civilian engineering, iron and steel, electric power, and basic chemicals. Those least favoured included consumer goods, housing, and agriculture.

According to this growth strategy, the latest available technologies were incorporated in large, newly built enterprises. But simultaneously, in view of the unsatisfied demand for goods of all kinds, managers have preferred to maintain old equipment in use for as long as possible, and as a result the rate of withdrawal and replacement of existing capital stock has been extremely low by international standards. This has led to the formation of a low-technology repair and maintenance sector of formidable proportions. It employs some 6 million people and has a stock of machine tools as large as that possessed by the entire engineering industry of Japan.

An example of a large proton synchrotron — a form of particle accelerator — at Serpukhov. (*SCR*)

Extensive development was achieved by the highly centralised system of non-market, administrative allocation of resources, which enforced the key priorities. Over several decades, a highly differentiated economic system has formed and consolidated. Soviet industry, and indeed the economy as a whole, can be viewed as a multilevel, pyramidlike structure. At the upper levels of the pyramid are enterprises in priority branches, usually large, with high-quality production equipment, material inputs, and human resources, including access to the most proficient research and development (R & D) facilities. Enterprises at the apex of the pyramid include those responsible for the rockets Gorbachev singled out for praise. At lower levels, the quality of resources diminishes; at the base, there are countless small, ill-equipped factories, including repair works that use labour-intensive techniques and produce at low levels of quality. This rigidly stratified economic structure possesses considerable inertia and resistance to change.

In these circumstances, it is not surprising that Soviet technology exhibits such striking contrasts. Western studies have shown that in some fields performance is respectable by international standards. Since the early 1930s, the defence industry has enjoyed the highest state priority and access to quality resources; not surprisingly, its comparative technological performance has been the most consistently successful. In space technology, the considerable strengths of Soviet technology are generally acknowledged. Certain priority civilian activities also perform well, including the production of some types of equipment for the energy and transport sectors. In a number of fields, the Soviet Union is a world leader and has sold licences for original technologies to leading Western companies. Examples include a range of metallurgical processes, welding equipment, and laser and surgical stapling technologies. Priority is

The control panel of an atomic power station (*SCR*)

108

an important factor, but it does not necessarily guarantee success. This is illustrated by the example of Soviet computers and micro-electronics, which have consistently lagged behind achievements in the West.

As a rule, in lower-priority fields the comparative technological performance is less impressive. The Prime Minister, Nikolai Ryzhkov, revealed in 1986 that fewer than 30 per cent of the batch-produced products of the civilian engineering industry (by no means the least privileged sector) were up to world technological levels. Relatively poor performance is also found in many industrial consumer goods industries, in food processing, and several other major industries, including building materials and paper. Thus, the Soviet technological level is very uneven; it lags behind the West in many sectors, but this is by no means a general rule. Two major determinants of Soviet technological performance are the R and D system and the innovation process by which ideas for new products and technologies are translated into reality.

THE RESEARCH AND DEVELOPMENT SYSTEM

The R and D system employs more than 1½ million scientists and teachers in higher education. It has three principal sectors (see Fig. 10). First, less than 10 per cent of those employed work in the prestigious Academies of Sciences of the USSR and the republics, but Academy institutes undertake a high proportion of Soviet

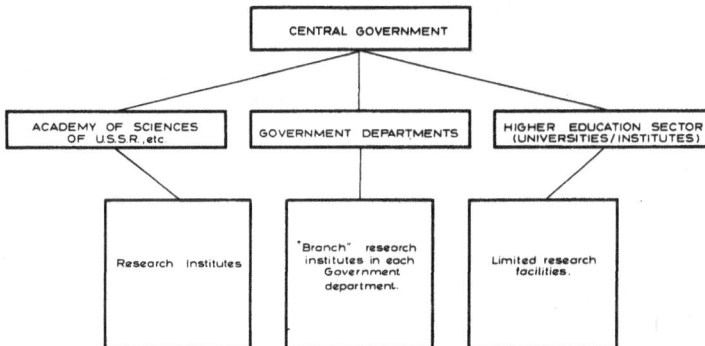

Figure 10   *Organisation of Soviet Science*

109

fundamental research. Second, almost 40 per cent are employed by universities and other higher educational establishments, but they account for a modest share — less than one-tenth — of the total research effort in terms of expenditure. Third, the remaining 50 per cent mainly work in 'branch' research organisations, thus designated because they are directly subordinate to industrial, agricultural and other ministries and government departments. This sector of Soviet science is responsible for most of the country's applied research and development.

The leading centre of Soviet science is the USSR Academy of Sciences, the origins of which date back to 1724. The Academy has approximately 750 full Academicians and 'corresponding members' (the latter have no voting rights), elected by secret ballot at general meetings of Academicians. Membership is considered a matter of great prestige in Soviet society. The Academy's day-to-day affairs are managed by its Presidium, which is chaired by the President, currently Yurii Marchuk who was elected to the post in 1986. The President of the Academy is the principal spokesman for Soviet scientific policy and is known to attend some Politburo meetings in an advisory capacity. Research is carried out in an extensive network of institutes, observatories and other establishments, some of which are concentrated in scientific centres, the most important being those of Novosibirsk, Leningrad, the Urals, and the Far East. All the republics, with the exception of the Russian Republic, have their own Academies, and some of their institutes make major contributions in particular fields of research and technology. The Ukrainian Academy, for example, is renowned for its successes with welding, special metallurgical processes, and super-hard materials.

An important policy issue facing the Academy has been the extent to which it should engage in research and development of direct practical benefit to the economy. During the early 1960s, in an attempt to focus its efforts on basic research supported by Khrushchev, many of the technically-oriented institutes were transferred to the industrial research network. During the 1980s, this policy has been reversed. Some of the transferred institutes have been returned to the Academy, and new institutes have been created in such fields as microelectronics, computing and machine building. Many of the republican academic institutes have always had a more practical orientation, with quite a high proportion of contract funding. But basic research generally is funded by grants from the state budget.

Yurii Marchuk, President of the Soviet Academy of Sciences (*Novosti*)

As noted earlier, the higher educational establishments employ a large proportion of the total number of scientists but make a modest contribution to the total research effort. The major universities of Moscow, Leningrad, Kiev, Novosibirsk and other prominent cities are exceptions, in so far as they have well-developed research facilities and undertake important basic and applied research. This also applies to a number of leading technical educational institutes, including the Moscow Bauman Higher Technical School, the Moscow Aviation Institute, and the Leningrad Polytechnic Insti-

111

View of Akademgorodok, the 'Science City' in West Siberia (*SCR*)

tute, the latter possessing the country's leading robotics research centre.

The largest component of the Soviet R and D system, the 'branch' sector, is responsible for a high proportion of the total applied research and development. At the beginning of 1987, of the 5070 scientific establishments in the country, 1550 were of an industrial profile, more than 900 were agricultural, and 200 served transport, communications and trade. Much of the work of this sector is undertaken on a contract basis; it is often financed by funds created from the profits of enterprises. In the past, the research institutes in this sector were subordinated directly to the ministries and, therefore, were often divorced from the practical concerns of production to the detriment of successful innovation. Since the late 1960s, this problem has been tackled by amalgamating institutes with enterprises to form science–production associations, the number of which in industry reached more than 330 by the beginning of 1987.

THE INNOVATION PROCESS AND ITS PROBLEMS

Expenditure on R and D has been impressive and compares favourably with the leading Western countries. It has been estimated that Soviet expenditure on R and D in 1982 amounted to approximately 3.7 per cent of GNP, compared with 2.7 per cent for the United States, 2.5 per cent for Japan, and an average of just over 2 per cent for the major West European countries. In absolute terms, expenditure in the same year was approximately 75 per cent of the U.S. level, but it has been estimated that the Soviet Union has approximately 50 per cent more research scientists and engineers than does the United States, and R and D expenditure is more than twice that of Japan. However, since the mid-1970s, the ratios have become less favourable to the USSR. During the 1960s and early 1970s, expenditure grew much more rapidly than in the United States and other major Western nations, but since 1975 it has grown more slowly.

The high level of expenditure does not ensure top quality research and trouble-free innovation; some of the problems arise within science itself. In many fields, Soviet scientists are inadequately supplied with the latest high-quality research equipment, including computers. For this reason, Soviet strengths are often found in disciplines of a theoretical nature, the so-called 'blackboard' sciences, which are not dependent on advanced instrumentation. Difficulties also arise from the structure of the research institutes, which tend to be hierarchical and inflexible. When the rate of growth of scientific personnel declined during the 1970s and research staff began to age, these problems became even more serious. By the end of the Brezhnev period, many institutes were dominated by veteran scientists; in the absence of accepted retirement procedures, they clung to their posts and privileges, blocking the promotion prospects of younger colleagues. By 1986, a mere 0.6 per cent of the Academicians in the USSR Academy of Sciences were younger than 50; 37 per cent were older than 75, and many of these individuals were institute directors who dominated major fields of research. A further weakness of the research system is that institutes are guaranteed funding almost regardless of their research contribution. There is truth in the old Soviet adage that it is easier to discover a new element than close down a research laboratory.

Even more serious problems are encountered as research findings are translated into new products and processes. Many R and D establishments lack adequate experimental production facilities, and organisational barriers keep institutes divorced from industry. As noted earlier, the science–production association has been promoted as a solution to these problems. But this form of organisation has not always proved appropriate, and some scientists fear that in time the routine demands of production will erode their research potential. The successful implementation of large R and D projects involving organisations of different ministries is frequently frustrated by departmentalism and the absence of effective means of coordination.

In the West, a distinction is sometimes drawn between 'science push' and 'demand pull' innovations. With science push innovation, new technologies and products are generated within the R and D sector and then 'sold' to industry for commercialisation. With demand pull innovations, a market opportunity is detected and research is then initiated to meet the demand. In practice, successful innovation often requires the effective coupling of both the research and the market dimensions. In the Soviet economy, most innovation arises from science push. Customer pull is usually weak or completely absent; the only major exception to this rule is the defence sector, where the armaments industry has a strong, demanding customer in the Ministry of Defence. This weakness of customer

Space mission control centre — the first stage of the Venus–Halley's comet international project, 1986. (*SCR*)

power is a major factor accounting for unsatisfactory innovation in the Soviet civilian economy.

In view of the inadequate pressure of demand for technological novelty, industrial enterprises often have little interest in making new products or in introducing the latest production processes. There are special incentives to promote innovative activity, but these are often insufficient to counteract the disadvantages of innovation, which tends to disrupt current production and, therefore, to reduce the normal bonuses earned from the successful fulfilment of delivery contracts. In priority sectors of the economy, there is usually not only greater pressure for innovation but also a superior capability in terms of technical and managerial skills, supported by better rewards for successful work.

A characteristic feature of the Soviet economy is the relatively slow rate of diffusion of new technologies throughout industry, following an initial application at a pioneer enterprise. The steel industry provides good examples. The USSR pioneered the continuous casting process now widely used in many countries; some of the installations in Japan and elsewhere were based on Soviet licences. But in the Soviet Union itself the share of steel cast using this technology is lower than in most major steel-producing

115

countries. Such low diffusion rates can be explained not only by the usual problems facing any innovation but also by shortcomings of the planning system and by conservatism. They are further exacerbated by the delays in project completion characteristic of the Soviet construction industry and by the modest rate of withdrawal of old production technologies (described earlier). Regarding the latter point, the experience of the steel industry is again instructive. Almost half of all steel is smelted by the open-hearth process, and this is no longer employed in Japan and other countries.

Before dealing with the recent reforms, it is worth considering briefly some other institutions concerned with Soviet science policy. The State Committee for Science and Technology (SCST), the current chairman of which is B. L. Tolstykh, plays an important role in determining technology policy, in selecting projects, and in overseeing R and D programmes of national importance. It is also responsible for the elaborate network of organisations concerned with scientific and technical information. The inventions and patents system, which was run by a separate state committee until 1987, now also comes under the overall leadership of the SCST.

A feature of Soviet science is the emphasis placed on the promotion of voluntary participation in R and D activities. The All-Union Society of Inventors and Rationalisers, sponsored by the trade unions, claims a multimillion membership, as does the network of Scientific and Technical Societies. The All-Union Znanie (Knowledge) Society popularises science through lectures and publications, the latter including the popular monthly *Nauka i Zhizn'* (*Science and Life*) with a print run of more than 3 million copies.

A review of the Soviet R and D system is incomplete without consideration of the role of the Communist Party. Approximately half of all the scientists and one-quarter of the engineers are members of the Party. The Central Committee Secretariat has a Science and Education Department that seeks to ensure that Party policies in these fields are implemented; it also plays an active role in shaping new policies and in selecting leading personnel.

Relations between the Party and the scientists have not always been smooth. The notorious Lysenko affair, when the Party gave its backing to the spurious theory of inheritance advocated by Trofim Lysenko on the grounds that it allegedly conformed to the precepts of Marxist–Leninist philosophy, caused lasting harm to Soviet genetics and to Soviet biology in general. In the Brezhnev period, when the Science Department was headed by the conservative historian S. P. Trapeznikov, there were arbitrary interventions in science that had especially harmful consequences for the develop- ment of the social sciences. However, on the other side, it must be stressed that the Party leadership has placed considerable emphasis over the years on the role of science and technology in the development of socialist society and has made available substantial resources for their growth.

REFORM AND MODERNISATION

Since the death of Brezhnev, and especially since Gorbachev was elected General Secretary, efforts have been made to revitalise the R and D system and create conditions for more rapid technological innovation. The reforms that are being introduced affect all the main components of the R and D system.

The need to boost Soviet basic research capability is strongly stressed. In the Academy of Sciences, measures adopted to date include the introduction of age limits for directors of institutes: 70 for full and corresponding members of the Academy and 65 for others. At the same time, a policy of appointing and promoting younger scientists is being actively pursued. More emphasis is being placed on the production and, if necessary, importation of up-to- date laboratory equipment. There has also been pressure for a democratisation of the Academy, including the right of institute staffs to elect their own directors instead of the traditional system of election from above.

Similar developments are taking place in the higher educational sector, where there is a new emphasis on the need to produce graduates with the knowledge and skills appropriate to modern conditions. An attempt is being made to upgrade the skills of teachers and to increase their involvement in research activity. Greater emphasis is to be placed on contract research for industry, with improved financial incentives for staff participation. Higher degrees are to be linked more directly to the needs of the economy.

The system of branch research organisations is now being rationalised. Some have been closed down; others have merged with enterprises to form new science–production associations. In this

117

sector, there is a strong emphasis on the need for R and D establishments to operate on a profit-and-loss basis, with a heavy reliance on contract funding and improved incentives for successful innovation. Here, and indeed more generally in Soviet science, there is to be a new emphasis on competitive tendering for projects.

Other new developments are equally striking. Temporary R and D groups are envisaged for specific new technology projects. One of the first, based in Novosibirsk, is for the development of a new supercomputer. Inter-branch scientific and technical complexes are being established; these unite institutes and enterprises from different ministries for top-priority, national R and D programmes. By the end of 1987, there were already about 25 of these complexes in such fields as industrial lasers, personal computers, robotics, membrane technologies, and biotechnology.

Reform of the R and D system alone will not solve the problems of Soviet science and technology; the 'new economic mechanism' also has a vital role to play. The new Soviet concept is that the relaxation of rigid forms of directive planning, coupled with an extension of market relations and a new emphasis on profitability and flexible prices, will promote a Soviet version of an 'enterprise culture' more favourable to risk taking and innovation. In principle, the new system should lead to a strengthening of customer power and also permit easier access to foreign markets. The new scope for joint ventures with Western firms should also assist the modernisation process.

In considering the prospects for the future, the broader dimensions of the *perestroika* must be borne in mind. The Gorbachev reforms strongly emphasise the 'human factor', democratisation, and *glasnost'*. For success in revitalising Soviet science and improving technological capability, these political, social and cultural changes may prove to be at least as important as the narrower issues already discussed in this chapter. The loss of morale and self-esteem in large sections of the intelligentsia, and indeed in society at large, was one of the most depressing legacies of the Brezhnev period. At the time of writing there are signs of a change for the better, and this could be an important factor in the ultimate success of the reform. Although it is unlikely that Gorbachev will be able to announce that the technological superiority of socialism has been proved, he may be in a position to claim credit for keeping the Soviet Union in the league of major industrial countries.

9

Farms and Farmers

R. E. F. SMITH

R. E. F. SMITH

PEASANT FARMING

As discussed in Chapter 1, the land and climate of the USSR does not favour farming. Only a quarter of the area can be tilled, compared with about two-thirds in the United States of America. The country is subject to extremes of cold, heat, and moisture, and this variation makes much of the area impossible to farm. It is true that in the south of European Russia and stretching eastwards, virtually to the Great Wall of China, there are fertile, black-earth soils. But this region of the steppes is exposed to considerable dangers of drought. Altogether, the continental nature of the country means that the moderating effect of the sea on climate is much less than in Western Europe. The range of temperatures is increased and the frost-free period is restricted. Even in those areas where it is possible to farm, the work period, that is the period when farmers can get on to the land, is limited, and there are long months when virtually nothing can be done outside. This contributes to a tendency to work in spurts at key periods, with lengthy intervening periods of idleness.

The title of this chapter is in some ways misleading. In one sense, farmers have never been important in Russia. The term *farmer* implies a man who works the land in order to market the produce. The peasant, as distinct from the farmer, is not necessarily closely tied to the market; his prime concern is not to market produce in order to get money from his land, but rather to maintain himself and his family directly from the land. If he makes money, it is used to meet tax and other demands; for him, money is just a different sort of crop with its own set of use values. Russian farming traditionally has been 'peasant farming'. There is, even today, a considerable feeling for this historical fact; members of Soviet collective farms are often referred to in the Soviet Union as 'collective farm peasantry' rather than 'collective farmers'. We must take account of Russia's history to understand farming in today's Soviet Union.

At the time of the First World War, five-sixths of the Russian population lived in the countryside, and it was not until the 1950s that more than half the population of the Soviet Union lived in towns. The vast majority of people living in the countryside at the time of the First World War lived on family farms. They worked the land with family labour; only occasionally was there a hired man. The peasants lived, for the most part, in fairly small villages, in wooden houses with thatched or shingled roofs. The land was still worked, as in medieval Britain, in the form of scattered strips that were reallocated between families from time to time. Consequently, the highest unit of peasant organisation was very often the commune — a group of people on a particular territory who came together, whether they lived in one village or more than one village, to divide up a particular area of land so that each family should have what was felt to be a fair share. This central function of dividing up the land, which was in short supply owing to rapid growth of population, was quite crucial and held the peasant community together against the outside world, even where there were fierce internal arguments about every inch of land.

From the viewpoint of the national economy, peasant farming of this type had major drawbacks. The peasants' lack of concern to market produce meant there was very little possibility for state accumulation of capital and, hence, for industrialisation. In the period between the 1905 and 1917 Revolutions, a series of agrarian reforms had been carried through (named after the Prime Minister of the time, Stolypin) that encouraged peasants to withdraw from the commune and to set up as individual farmers with consolidated holdings or at least enclosed fields. By 1917, a certain tendency to leave the commune was already marked, at least on paper, but one should not exaggerate the impact of the Stolypin reforms. In 1917, simultaneously with the two political revolutions described in Chapter 2, a third revolution (an agrarian one) took place; this was an elemental movement throughout the countryside, in the course of which the peasants seized and often reallocated land taken from the large landowners, the church, the estates, and even from wealthier peasants. They divided up this land among themselves, and the old communal institutions were strengthened almost everywhere.

A village scene in the Gor'kii region (*SCR*)

The Bolsheviks had come to power in 1917, but there was a major contradiction that was not resolved till the 1930s, and even then the resolution itself posed further problems. The problem was this: the land was now in peasant hands, but the peasant outlook, because it was not market-directed, was basically one that could manage without the state. For its part, however, the state could not manage without the peasants. The state demanded peasant surpluses to accumulate the wealth needed to undertake the intended reforms: to recover from the disasters of the First World War and to build a modernised Russia that would no longer suffer the ills of backwardness. The peasants, however, had basically what might be regarded as anarchistic views. In fact, insofar as there was any peasant political movement, it was represented by groups whose colour is now virtually forgotten; not for them either reds or whites, they were the original greens. Their views resulted in a desire for local republics. They were dominated by local parochial interests and not concerned

121

with the formation of those larger units that are essential to the political administration of a great land empire such as Russia. The peasants were organised in about 20 million farms, and each of these was inclined to go its own way. If they came together, they came together for specific local purposes, such as allocating land, building a bridge, erecting a school or church, or choosing a herdsman to pasture the cattle or a watchman to guard against fire.

The state, for its part, had to obtain food supplies and other raw materials, and 1918–21 was a period when the state administration had virtually no foothold in the countryside. Armed squads had to be sent from the towns to collect grain, and only gradually was this state banditry against the mass of the population changed into a more regular taxation system in kind. In fact, not until the mid-1920s, ten years after the Revolution of 1917, did Soviet power begin to have an effective hold on the countryside; and this effective hold, of course, was not always seen by the peasants as being in their interests.

From the earliest days of the Bolshevik Revolution, there had been encouragement for the formation of collectives in the countryside — what were called communes (*kommuny*), 'artels' (groups of work-ers), and cooperatives of various sorts were all encouraged. It was felt that rather than the individualistic, and therefore potentially capitalistic, entrepreneurial approach of the Russian peasantry, collective activities were likely to coincide much more with the Bolshevik view of the world and the state. But these collective units that were encouraged were rather like some of those communes that exist at present in this country, or used to in the interwar years. They were, for the most part, groups not of land workers, but of intellectuals, people who either wanted to 'opt out' of the real world as they found it or regarded a 'back to the land' movement as their contribution to the struggle against Russia's backwardness.

Peasants, for their part, were uninterested in the politics of the state organisations; they were uninformed and uncomprehending about what was going on around them. This is scarcely surprising. The majority of the people of the countryside were still illiterate before the mid-1920s. Even quite simple newspapers frequently had to be read to people in the countryside, and some of the new terms introduced and the new terms of speech being used by the cosmopolitan intellectuals who had carried through the Revolution of 1917 meant absolutely nothing to the peasants. A characteristic story is that at the time when the first tractors were being introduced in the countryside, peasants did not understand the difference between *tractorist* and *Trotskyist*.

For its part, the state laid great hopes on the organisation of larger units in the countryside. The very limited quantity of machinery available could be used most effectively if there were large fields to be worked. The traditional small strips farmed by the poorer peasants were quite unsuitable for tractor cultivation; and, added to that, it was the larger and richer peasant families who supplied most of the surplus. But these richer peasant families, these successful farmers, who in England would have been regarded as *yeomen* (a word of approval) were regarded with fear and apprehension by the Bolsheviks because they were seen as potential capitalists. These men were called *kulaks* (tight fists). The Bolshevik use of the word *kulak* is really a distortion of its original meaning. Originally, to the peasants, it meant not so much the tight-clenched fist as the cupped hand in which smaller men are held. They may be held in an oppressive grip or a protective one; there is an ambiguity about the term in its original meaning. The Bolsheviks came to use it simply to mean the oppressive and threatening fist of emergent capitalism in the countryside.

COLLECTIVE FARMS AND STATE FARMS

But Bolshevik hopes for large-scale farming and fears of emergent capitalism met with little response from the peasants. The Bolshevik collectivisation campaign at the beginning of the 1930s met with intense peasant resistance. Some of its economic and social consequences are discussed in Chapter 3.

What was a collective farm? It was basically a cooperative farm, in which individual peasant farms were amalgamated into larger units. But it was a cooperative with a difference — an organisational arrangement forced on the peasant, in an economy not fully based on money and with poorly developed links between farms and the market. The collective farms were organised so that most of the land was worked jointly, and much of the produce of this collective land was delivered compulsorily to the state at very low prices. The collective-farm members did not receive wages, merely a share of produce remaining after the compulsory deliveries had been met. The share-out was not on an egalitarian basis but was determined

123

according to the number of conventional labour-days that each farm member had worked. The actual days worked did not coincide with the labour-days; for instance, a skilled worker (e.g. a lorry driver) would obtain several labour-days for each actual day worked, whereas a woman sweeping out a yard would receive only a fraction of a labour-day for a full day's work. The amount paid out for each labour-day was an appropriate fraction of the produce retained by the farm. In this way, wage payments were avoided, and the countryside continued to maintain itself while considerable quantities of produce were handed over to the state at low prices.

The collective-farm member did not spend his whole time working the collective land. At first, some Communists had argued that not only the fields but also the livestock, the houses, and the eating arrangements should be made communal. Some of those against collectivisation accused the Communists of even proposing to communalise wives. In the end, it was decided that the fields and some of the livestock should be jointly held and worked, but that each family should also retain its own house and a garden, a garden

A collective farm market in a Soviet city

124

usually of some size by British standards, which would enable the collective-farm members to have not only flower-beds and a kitchen garden but also orchards and a few animals. In fact, until quite recently, these personal plots of the individual farm families were the main source of everything except the major field crops (mostly grain), including most vegetables and milk. In the hard years of the 1930s, the peasant could not have survived without the personal plot, and most of his income in money came from the sale on the market of produce grown on this plot.

A further important aspect of the collective farm was the existence of state-owned Machine-Tractor Stations (MTS). When collective farming was first instituted on a mass scale in the 1930s, peasants killed millions of their livestock. The slaughter of horses was particularly important because, as we have to remind ourselves continually, until the 1930s, horse-drawn implements (including the traditional forked tillage implement, the *sokha*) were used almost

Teaching peasants the workings of a tractor. Scene on a Machine Tractor Station in the 1930s. (*SCR*)

everywhere in Russia. Not all peasant households of that time had even this very simple implement. There were only 1 million threshing machines in the country and 3 million reapers. The first MTS were organised in 1929. They were state-run agricultural contractor services that supplied machinery and the men to work the machinery to farms on contract; but they also supervised, and partly controlled, collective farms. The collective farm had to supply a further substantial sum of money or grain to the MTS in return for their services. In the first years after collectivisation in the 1930s, the tractor power available was too small to make good the loss in horses killed.

Agriculture had not fully recovered from the disaster caused by collectivisation before the German invasion of the Second World War. The war caused immense losses to Russian agriculture. It was followed by a period of very strict control of the collective farms, which lasted until after Stalin's death in 1953. Punitive taxation was retained, and the private plots held by individual members of the farm were reduced in size. In 1950, a campaign was started to reduce the number of collective farms by amalgamating them. The aim was to create more easily mechanised units. There were about a quarter of a million collective farms in 1950; in two years, the number fell to 97 000 and there are now about 27 000. This means that collective farms these days are very large, often including four or five villages within their boundaries. In fact, they are by no means what we would regard as a farm, but something much more akin to a parish or area organised within a planned economy as a single agricultural-producing unit. Many farms, in fact, include some local industry within their boundaries. This is one reason why it is more accurate to talk about collective-farm members rather than collective farmers. In units of their size, there are obviously going to be many people who provide services but do not farm the land.

After Stalin's death in 1953, Khrushchev introduced many new measures affecting agriculture. Prices for agricultural produce were raised and taxation was reduced. The part played by the MTS was changed, and a little later their equipment was sold off to individual collective farms. An enormous campaign was undertaken in which 36 million hectares of new land was ploughed up, mainly in southern Siberia and northern Kazakhstan. This tremendous extension of the sown area was intended to offset the continuing insecure basis of farming in Russia. It did not deal with the weakness of crop growing in Russia by intensifying farming. There are, of course, immense reserves in intensification, but such a policy would, inevitably, involve very considerable capital investment. More fertilisers, new machinery and new types of seed would be needed, along with a considerable investment in raising the general level, including the educational level, of people in the countryside.

The disasters that have struck the countryside and the great stress that has been put on industrialisation in the Soviet Union have resulted in a situation something like that in Ireland: most of the lively lads have left the countryside for the town. In the Irish case, however, the town happens to be overseas; in the Russian case, the town is internal, but the result is that, in the main, the less strong, less adventurous, and less enterprising people have been left in the countryside. The decision to extend the sown area, therefore, was conceived as a simple and relatively easy way of increasing the total crop. But it was really only after the Khrushchev period (from the late 1960s) that farm produce began to receive prices that were at all

Women working inside a collective farm (*SCR*)

127

reasonable. From this period on, many collective-farm members also began to receive wages and pension rights. The money basis of farming was extended. Collective farms in the USSR continue to be subject to considerable control from above, from the local councils (the soviets) and planning bodies, from ministries who purchase their produce, and from the Communist Party in the countryside. But they do have a much greater degree of initiative, and they are much more a part of the total society than they have ever been.

A substantial part of Soviet agriculture is organised not into collective farms but into state farms. State farms are directly controlled by the state, and those who work on them receive a wage. There has been a noticeable increase in the number of state farms since the 1960s. Of course, when collective farmers become wage earners there is much less difference between collective and state farms. Moreover, it is no doubt convenient from the point of view of the state to have the direct control that results from the organisation of a state farm.

Since the mid-1960s, and especially from about 1980, considerable changes have been made in the administrative framework of agriculture. Recently, under Gorbachev, the problems of high, and largely unrecognised, subsidies to food production (a result of large state investments) and uneconomically low food prices to the consumer are beginning to be tackled. The agricultural sector (now known as the Agro–Industrial Complex) is organised for planning purposes as a unity covering the production, storage, and processing of, and trade in, its output, as well as its direct supply requirements. Farms, both collective and state, are encouraged to form associations with one another, with industrial plants processing their produce and with farm suppliers; they have also been given some independence in decision making within the planning system. In a variety of different areas, experiments with 'family contracts' and other devices are placing new emphasis on the role of the family as a production unit. Are these measures, perhaps, a step toward something similar to the agricultural sector in Western countries? A reason formally given for these measures is to increase food supplies to the population, as envisaged in the Food Programme agreed to in 1982. That document claims that 'everywhere the populace has an uninterrupted supply of bread, rolls, pasta products and sugar'. Many visitors to the Soviet Union will appreciate the truth of this — and the significance of what is not claimed.

AGRICULTURE TODAY

What have been the results for agriculture of all these changes during the Soviet period? The crop structure of Russian farming has changed (see Fig. 11, Table 2). Grains have become less important relative to potatoes and vegetable crops; rye, despite an overall increase in the harvest of all grains, shows an absolute decrease. The growing of wheat has been increased and extended into west Siberia and Kazakhstan; oats have declined as machines have replaced horses. Yields of grain have, since the time of the First World War (see Fig. 12), virtually doubled (see Table 2). Potato yields and yields for vegetables have increased greatly only in the last few years (see Fig. 13). Crop farming, then, has shown noticeable advances, achieved partly through an extension of the sown area and carried out with a considerable reduction in the numbers employed in agriculture.

Livestock, however, continues to be the weakest aspect of farming in Russia. The hay yields are perhaps no more than one-tenth of those regarded as acceptable in this country; yet animals have to be stalled for about 200 days each year. In 1917, root crops were virtually unknown, and animals had to be fed on straw and coarse feeds. In times of famine, the thatch had to be taken off the peasant houses to keep the animals alive. During the Soviet period, there has certainly been a substantial improvement in fodder supplies, though they still remain poor by standards in Western Europe or the United States (see Table 3). By the late 1920s, livestock numbers had, in general, recovered to the level on the eve of the First World War. But the collectivisation programme of the 1930s resulted in mass slaughter of livestock. Recovery was encouraged by the fairly wide use of artificial insemination, but the invasion by Nazi Germany took place before livestock numbers had reached their pre-collectivisation levels. Recently, substantial advances are noticeable, in both the number of animals (see Fig. 14) and their productivity.

Overall, since 1917, Russian farming has radically changed, as the country has moved from an agrarian to an industrialised situation (see Table 4). Concealed unemployment on the land has been virtually eliminated by the growth of industrial employment, but this industrialisation was initially carried through at the expense of farming. The countryside was given a very low priority in

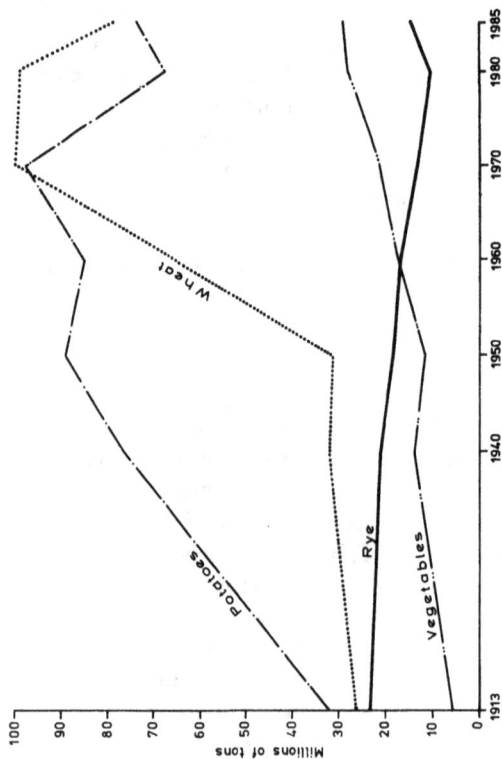

Figure 11 *Output of selected grains, 1913-1985*

Table 2 *Harvest (millions of tons) and yields (centners per hectare)*

	1913		1940		1950		1960		1970		1980		1985	
grains	86.0	8.2	95.6	8.6	81.2	7.9	125.5	10.9	186.8	15.6	189.1	14.9	191.7	16.2
rye	23.2	8.0*	21.1	9.1*	18.0	7.6*	16.4	10.1	13.0	13.0	10.2	11.8	15.7	16.6
wheat	27.3	10.0*	31.8	10.1*	31.1	9.1*	64.3	15.1*	99.7	22.8*	98.2	22.1*	78.1	21.6*
		7.3+		6.6+		7.6+		9.5+		12.3+		12.4+		12.1+

* – Winter sown   + – Spring sown

130

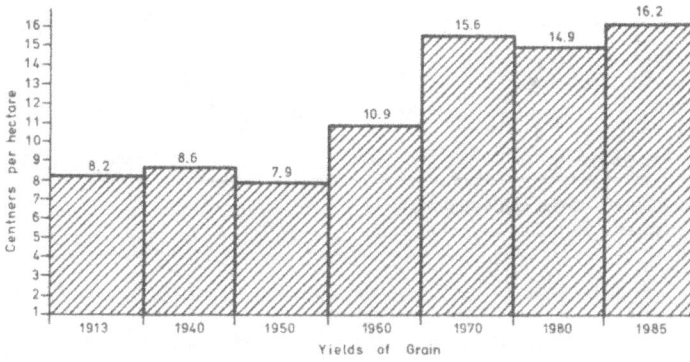

Figure 12   *Grain yields, 1913–1985*

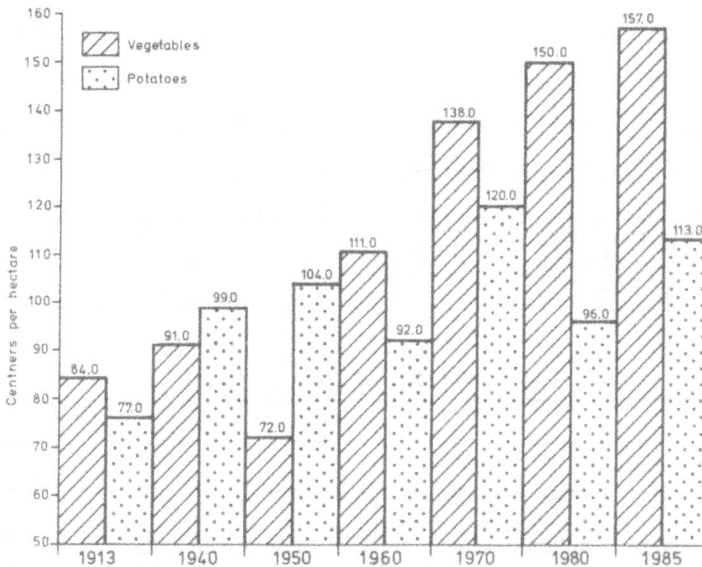

Figure 13   *Yields of vegetables and potatoes, 1913–1985*

131

Table 3   Harvest of feed crops (million tons)

	1940	1960	1970	1980	1985
hay and green feed including from	75.0	94.6	110.3	148.0	185.0
natural meadows	60.7	43.2	49.5	49.3[a]	59.2[b]
roots	12.4	17.8	35.7	41.6	59.0
maize for silage and used green		315	212	266	331

[a] Includes 2.7 from cultivated pastures
[b] Includes 3.5 from cultivated pastures

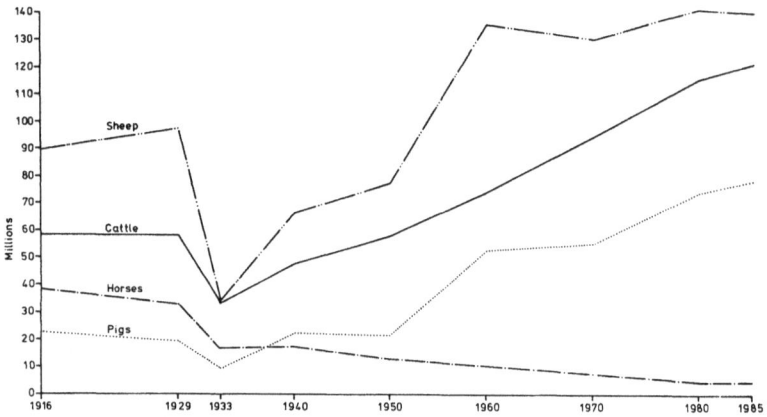

Figure 14   Livestock numbers, 1916–1985

Table 4   Numbers of socialised farms, population and tractors

	1913	1928	1940	1950	1960	1970	1985
collective farms, all types (thousands)	—	33.3	236.9	123.7	44.9	33.0	26.2
state farms (thousands)	—	1.4	4.2	5.0	7.4	15.0	22.7
total population (millions)	159.2	150.6	194.1	178.5	212.3	241.7	276.3
rural population (millions)	130.7	123.0	131.0	109.1	108.5	105.7	96.2
tractors (million horse-power)	—	0.5	17.6	27.7	47.6	111.6	230.0
tractors (thousand physical units)	—	27.0	531.0	595.0	1122.0	1977.0	2775.0

Harvesting the fields by modern methods (*SCR*)

development plans. The change from largely traditional strip farming with simple wooden implements to large-scale tractor farming has involved the formation of collective farms and state farms and the elimination of the individual family farm. Only in recent years has farming, as a whole, been put on anything like a par with other sectors of the economy, and it is only in this period that agricultural production has substantially increased.

The continued insecurity of Soviet crop farming is reflected in a Soviet witticism. Lenin's famous definition of Communism as 'Soviet power plus electrification' has now become 'Soviet power

133

Table 5(a) Per capita consumption (kg./year) of selected items
(a – urban, b – average for USSR, c – rural population)

		Grain	Potatoes	Fruit and vegetables	Meat and animal products	Fish	Milk and milk products	Sugar	Vodka and spirits (litres of absolute alcohol)
1913	b	200	114	51	29	6.7	154	8.1	
1940*	b	490	390		24	7.3	172	11	
1940	b	202	135	46	16		142	2.5	
1950	b	200	241	62	26	7.0	172	11.6	
1960	a	139	117	127	49.4		253	39.2	
	b	164	143	92	39.5	9.9	240	28.0	3.8
	c	188	168	59	30.0		228	17.3	
1970	a	135	117	163	58		350	45	
	b	149	130	117	47.5	15.4	307	38.8	6.8
	c**	172	151	65	37.1		268	33.0	
1980	b	138	109	135	57.6	17.6	314	44.4	8.7
1985	b	133	104	150	61.7	18.0	325	42.2	7.2

*Production **1968
Underlined figures are estimates

Table 5(b)   Consumer durables, per thousand population (items)

		Watches and clocks	Radio	TV	Camera	Refrigerator or freezer	Washing machine	Motor cycle or scooter	Motor car	Bicycle	Sewing machine
1970	a	1463	237	185	110	132	195	15		132	173
	b	1193	199	143	77	89	141	21	6	145	161
	c	836	149	88	33	34	71	29		163	146
1980	a	1739	276	278	119	302	235	19	30	122	189
	b	1523	250	249	91	252	205	29	30	144	190
	c	1152	206	200	43	167	158	47	27	183	191
1985	a	1770	309	314	128	309	235	26	45	135	189
	b	1580	289	293	102	275	205	43	45	165	190
	c	1239	254	255	52	217	164	77	43	224	195

Table 5(a) gives some idea of the broad changes in the diets of Russian countryfolk over the Soviet period. The diet has been modernised. There is less grain consumed, and more fruit, vegetables, and meat, at least some of lower quality (Soviet animals produced in batteries are no better than ours). The consumption of milk and milk products has more than doubled. More than ten times as much sugar is consumed as in 1940; much of it consumed in the form of alcohol. Although Gorbachev's anti-alcohol campaign appears to be making some impact, we do not know how much illicit alcohol is being made.

Table 5(b) shows the substantial increase in consumer goods available in the countryside that took place in the Brezhnev years.

plus Canadian wheat'. But one has to point to the fact that despite the creation of Soviet Russia in hostile conditions, despite the intervention in the early years, the massive blunder of collectivisation, and the disasters of the Second World War, Russian farming has proved itself sufficiently viable to maintain the vast industrialisation programme that has been carried through. By concentrating all their efforts, the Russians were able to give us the word *Sputnik*; but at the same time, that concentration, that single-minded devotion to the development of an industry that was going to catch up and overtake the industrial West, probably resulted, until the last decade, in the town–country split in Russia being as wide as ever. This split is by no means closed. Moreover, comparison of per capita consumption in the seven Comecon countries about 1980 shows that the USSR was last for meat and meat products, second for milk and sugar, fifth for eggs and for vegetables, and fourth for cereals and for potatoes. It generally had the lowest yields of all these countries. All this raises the fundamental question: Have the efforts to industrialise been worthwhile from the point of view of the mass of the Russian population?

10

The Education of the Soviet Citizen

JOHN DUNSTAN

If a Westerner were so naive as to ask a Soviet official if there were any privileged classes in the USSR, the answer might be, 'Yes. There is one privileged class in our country — the children'. Clearly, the lavishly equipped 'palaces' and clubs, sports schools and centres, and art and music schools offer many young people unrivalled opportunities to follow any leisure-time activity that appeals to them. Of course, geographical factors make these activities a good deal more accessible in some areas than in others. But on principle the state regards its children as an investment and ploughs large sums into facilities for them. In time, these children will grow up and take part in the common task of building the new society. So the Party, as leader in the common task, does all in its power to develop their talents; partly for their own sakes, so that they can lead a full life, but particularly so that they can later make an ample contribution to the life of society. In so doing, the Party seeks to inculcate a sense of obligation intended to find expression in the utmost loyalty to itself, to the country, and to the Communist way of life. To this end, it works through the schools and other educational institutions, through young people's organisations, and, ideally, through the family.

ORIGINS AND DEVELOPMENT

Soviet education has developed under four main influences: Marxism–Leninism; Russian pedagogy of the 19th and early 20th centuries; Western European and American pedagogy of the early 20th century; and the social, political, and economic circumstances and needs confronting the Soviet state.

137

Although Marx, in his younger days, thought that the school would wither away along with the state, he later assumed its continued existence, at least for the time being. He explained the need for all-round education with intellectual, physical and technical components. The last of these had also been part of a utilitarian tradition in Russia dating back to Peter the Great. Tolstoy's stress on the free development of every child was upheld by his disciple S. T. Shatsky, who nevertheless sought a balance between individual rights and the reasonable demands of the children's community.

All these elements made their mark on education in the early Soviet period. The two key figures were Lunacharsky, the first People's Commissar of Education, and Krupskaya, Lenin's wife. They devised, in the Unified Labour School of 1918, a humanistic model of education that was essentially child-centred but still sensitive to the individual's social situation. The work of progressive educators like John Dewey was translated into Russian. It was by all accounts an exciting time. But an environment of civil war, famine, homelessness, poverty and general chaos was scarcely right for

Lunacharsky, People's Commissar for Education in the 1920s (*SCR*)

Lenin with his wife Nadezhda Krupskaya, their nephew Victor and another child in 1922 (*SCR*)

implementing idealistic educational theories. Things were often made worse by stick-in-the-mud teachers and by pupils who wanted to carry out their own little revolutions in the schools.

As early as 1920, the principle of combining maximum general education with a variety of work skills had been eroded by the necessity for earlier vocational training. Schools became increasingly vocationalised as the decade progressed. After the launching of the first five-year plan in 1928, there was much talk of merging schools into factories and farms, and some action resulted. In a final fling, radical educationists vociferously proclaimed the end of the school.

But the new era of industrialisation demanded stability and discipline, and general education of a very formal kind was firmly reinstated as the basis for specialised training. This was in 1931, the same year that the 'de-schoolers' were outlawed as 'leftist deviationists'.

During the 1930s, teachers and parents (in that order) acquired a new, responsible role. Earlier discussions about heredity and environment were largely superseded in theory, and as far as possible in practice, by emphasis on what was called a 'third factor' — purposeful upbringing. The seal was set on this in 1936 by the banning of 'pedology' (a Soviet form of child study) and intelligence testing, on the grounds that they assumed that the future of the child was fatalistically determined by heredity and environment. Upbringing was to occur in the setting of the children's collective or well-knit peer group. Under wise adult leadership, the collective would itself develop into an agent of upbringing, as its members learned purposeful self-discipline and the ability to put group interests above personal ones. These ideas and practices are associated with A. S. Makarenko. He pioneered the rehabilitation of young delinquents and waifs, using a vigorous no–nonsense approach that was accepted much better in the 1930s than in the 1920s. The product of purposive upbringing was the 'new man' (or, rather, new person), increasingly described as the 'new Soviet man', as patriotic education became more important with the rise of fascism in Europe and the German invasion of 1941.

Meanwhile, school was becoming more academic, achievement-oriented, and authoritarian. Standard curricula, syllabuses and textbooks were reintroduced. Homework assignments and examinations were reinstated, together with a four-point marking or grading system (later increased to five grades). The classroom lesson, conducted on a rigidly prescribed pattern, was the central feature. The central figure was the teacher, who was now supported by the youth organisations rather than subjected to their control as in the past. During the war years, this general approach was intensified.

There was, however, a remarkable interlude in policy between 1958 and the mid-1960s. Physical work, which had vanished from the general school in the 1930s, made a modest comeback in the mid-1950s. In 1958, the Khrushchev leadership included a massive amount of manual labour and vocational training in the timetable.

With an increasing shortage of production workers, the aim was to give youngsters a more positive attitude toward skilled jobs and to attract them away from higher education, where there were not enough openings. Students were also given practical work to do. But preparation for the 1958 reform was inadequate, and the reform was a disaster. The young people were overloaded, and those responsible could not cope; often, both academic and labour training were superficial. So in 1964 the curriculum was heavily pruned. Soon after this, Khrushchev and his 'harebrained schemes' were consigned to the dustbin of history. In 1966, vocational training in school ceased to be mandatory. The vaguer concept of physical work was substituted, for a mere two lessons a week throughout.

This modest arrangement was part of a reform that followed a two-year debate on the curriculum. The principle of this further reform was to reduce overloading and encourage efficient learning by reducing factual content and stressing key concepts. Greater efficiency would enable primary education to be reduced from four years to three. This provided an extra year for the middle stage, which thereby comprised forms (grades) four to eight of the ten-year school. Material could thus be moved down from the senior stage, making room there for additional concepts. Special interests were to be accommodated by options (electives).

Unfortunately, like Khrushchev's 1958 reform, the 1966 reform did not work well. The conceptual level was pitched too high, and a simultaneous campaign sought to give all young people the full ten years of general education. This meant that a very academic curriculum was being forced on more and more teenagers; they did not thrive on this diet. Meanwhile, young skilled workers continued to be in great demand; as a result, by the 1970s, the vocational aspect of education was once again back in the spotlight. In 1977, a decree pronounced that young people leaving the general school after completing the full ten years 'should have come near to mastering a specific occupation', and doubled labour training in the senior school years from two to four periods per week. A new wave of curriculum change shifted the emphasis away from theory to practical applications.

Following much further discussion, legislation for another major school reform was introduced in 1984. The most striking and controversial feature of this ambitious reform was the plan to double the proportion of 15-year-olds transferred to secondary vocational schools. This meant increasing the proportion from 30 to about 60 per cent, in the long run, and halving the proportion who stayed on for the senior stage of the general school. Less drastic changes have since been proposed. In the general school, an occupational skill was also to be acquired; the lesson time set aside for labour training and productive work was doubled. According to the reform, general and vocational schools would eventually be merged. A further feature was that the school starting age would be gradually lowered from seven to six, extending the whole course by a year to 11 years. Class sizes were to be reduced to 30 at the primary level (previously 40) and middle stage (previously 35), and to 25 at the senior level (previously 35). Other details are discussed later in this chapter.

Before long, however, it became clear that the reform was getting bogged down. In February 1988, the Party set the broad agenda for re-structuring the whole education system. Among other things, the general school is likely to increase its responsibilities for providing knowledge, not least as the basis for training in vocational schools. It will continue to develop a low-level occupational qualification at the senior stage only 'where conditions allow'. The structure, content and methods of general education are to become much more flexible and diversified. The details remain to be worked out. The three education ministries have been replaced by the new State Committee on Public Education.

THE CONTEMPORARY SCHOOL

What kind of school has been emerging in the course of these changes? (see Fig. 15) The following picture is based on the 1987–88 school year. Ivan Ivanovich Ivanov, better known as Vanya or Van'ka, and his twin sister Tanya start the general school at the age of six or seven. (Perhaps they will have received pre-school education; in 1984, these institutions catered for some 70 per cent of urban children and 35 per cent of rural children in the relevant age range.) Their school is coeducational and free. The primary course lasts four years, covering the usual basic subjects of Russian, mathematics, environment or nature study, art, singing, physical education, and also labour training. Perhaps Vanya and Tanya are at one of the growing number of so-called extended-day schools, or ordinary schools with extended-day facilities, which provides a hot

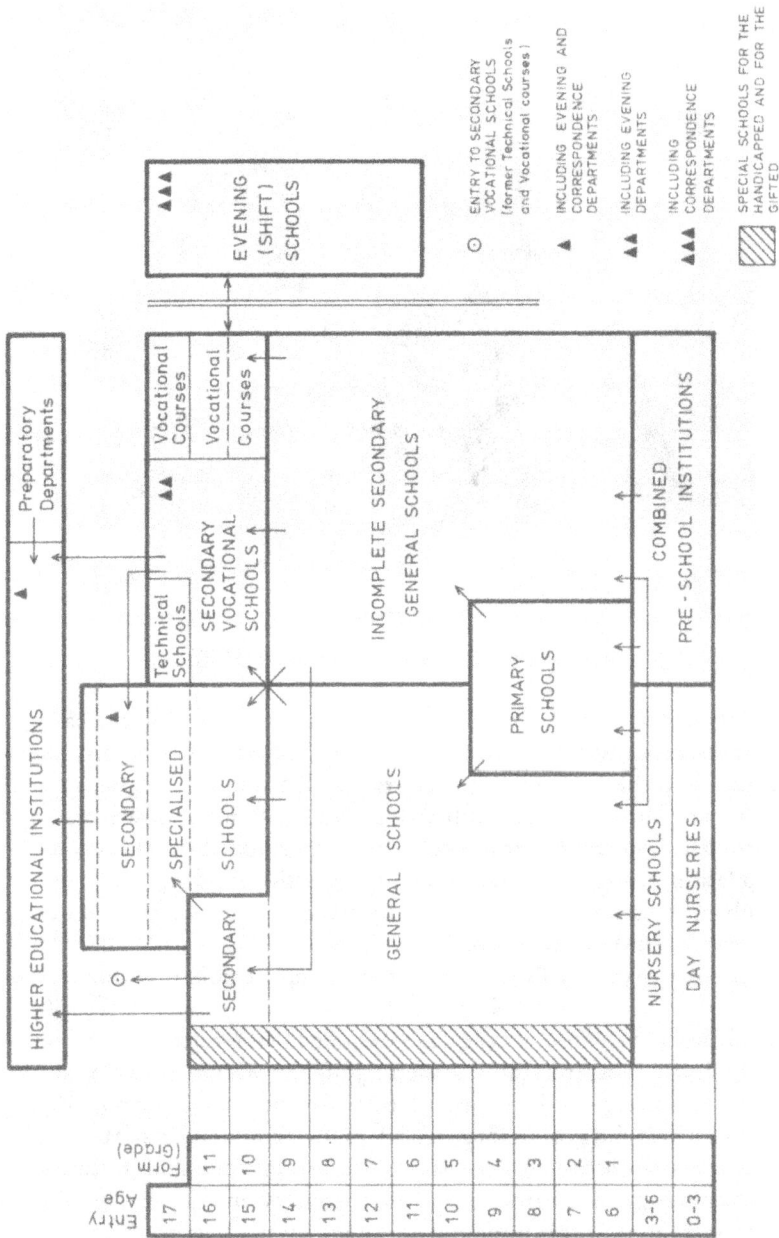

Figure 15 Simplified structure of the Soviet education system as at January 1988
(Note: the size of the boxes is not intended to represent student numbers)

A nursery for children of pre-school age (*SCR*)

dinner and supervised activities after lessons terminate in the early afternoon. In 1985, such arrangements covered 37 per cent of children in the first eight school years. All schools have afternoon meetings for hobbies and other activities; these may, however, be curtailed somewhat in districts where a shortage of school accommodation requires the working of a multi-shift day. They will probably join the Octobrists, an informal club for younger children rather like the Cub Scouts or Brownies.

When Vanya and Tanya are ten they enter form five, probably at the same school. The weekly workload goes up by six periods to 30, and history and a foreign language are added to the curriculum. Soon they will almost certainly want to join the Pioneers, the youth organisation for children aged 10 to 15, for they would be regarded as odd if they did not. In form six (11-plus), geography is started and biology is substituted for nature study. Physics and technical drawing begin in form seven and chemistry in form eight. For labour training at this middle stage, Vanya will do technical studies

144

and Tanya home economics, both of which include practical electricity. However, their country cousins, Sasha and Masha, spend 60 per cent of their labour training on agriculture, agricultural engineering, and practical electricity, not segregated by sex. From form seven onward, one period a week is devoted to a course on the principles of production and choosing a career. All pupils from forms five to ten must spend part of the summer doing continuous labour practice. To combat delinquency, a compulsory one-year course entitled 'Fundamentals of the Soviet State and Law' was introduced for 14-plus pupils in 1975. This will now be integrated with history and the senior-stage 'social studies' course (see next page). A similar course, 'Ethics and Psychology of Family Life', was instituted under the 1984 reform, straddling forms nine and ten and thus a possible move to another school.

At the end of form nine, at the age of about 15, Vanya and Tanya take examinations. At this point, they (1) stay on in the general secondary school if they aspire to higher education, or, if their school is only a nine-year one, proceed to another providing the two-year senior course; (2) enter a secondary specialised school with a three- or four-year course, which trains medium specialists in such fields as nursing, engineering or commerce, and includes senior-stage general education, though admission here is subject to further examination; or (3) enter a secondary vocational school that trains skilled workers using either a three-year course, which includes senior-stage general education, or a one- or two-year course without it. In the latter case, they will be expected to complete their general education on a part-time or evening basis, at a so-called evening (shift) school, or by correspondence. As will be seen later in this chapter, secondary vocational schools have many problems, and further change is to be expected.

The proportion of students choosing various paths was estimated in 1982 to be as follows: the senior classes of the general secondary schools, 61 per cent; specialised secondary schools, about 10 per cent; secondary vocational schools, 20 per cent; and other vocational schools, 8.5 per cent. The remaining 0.5 per cent at that time combined jobs with evening (shift) school attendance.

If Vanya and Tanya stay on in the general school, proceeding to form ten (15-plus), they continue nearly all the subjects of the ninth year. They embark on two-year courses in a specific occupation, leading to an initial trade qualification (though this will no longer be

145

Azerbaidzhani children at a
general school (*SCR*)

mandatory), and in computer studies. Vanya also does preliminary military training for two periods a week while Tanya concentrates on first aid. Form 11 sees the introduction of one-year courses in astronomy and 'social studies', in effect, a mixture of economics and civics treated, of course, in the appropriate ideological manner. This is the only part of the school curriculum in which the doctrines of Marxism-Leninism are formally taught, but they are implicit in the teaching of all subjects, though in some more than others because of the nature of the subjects.

Finally, there is provision for optional extras, rising from two hours a week in form 7 to four hours in form 11. By 1983, 91.5 per cent of youngsters in these forms were taking optional courses. They can sometimes be very effective: of 21 school leavers who had taken the option called 'Fundamentals of Television' at a Moscow school, 17 decided to make their careers in radio–electronics. But these courses have problems: they depend on the ability and enthusiasm of staff and the availability of visiting teachers; they are liable to turn into cramming sessions for pupils aiming at higher education, or remedial sessions for the floundering students; and they are also vulnerable when officialdom seeks more time for compulsory subjects.

To complete the picture, mention must also be made of the special schools for children gifted in the arts, sports, languages, mathematics and physics, and the special intensive classes in certain schools. In the early 1980s, all these schools together did not exceed 3 per cent of those providing ten-year general education. According to the 1984 reform, however, more pupils in the top four years are to be offered intensive teaching in various specialisms with the help of options. And in 1988 this 'differentiation' of the educational structure — by subject areas and by types of school — seemed set for further expansion. The traditional forms of provision for special interests and abilities are subject societies and clubs. There are also boarding schools, facilities for deprived children and those living in rural areas remote from schools, and special schools for the handicapped.

If we were to look in on Vanya and Tanya's class, at whatever level, the chances are that we would find the atmosphere strangely formal and well-disciplined, yet with a friendly relationship between teacher and pupils. One is slightly hesitant about generalising because foreign visitors are naturally shown the best schools. In the Soviet press, one sometimes comes across blackboard jungles or the occasional over-regimented school, but it would be rash to make too much of this; such public exposure is one Soviet way of remedying abuses. The authorities have an interest in turning out self-disciplined citizens who have conscientious but cheerful attitudes toward their work and their associates; this is reflected in the normal attitudes and practices of the school.

Academically, the average Soviet school seems in some ways to have more in common with the traditional English grammar school than with many schools of our day. The stress is on talk, chalk, textbooks, hard work, and achievement. Indeed, concern is still expressed that Soviet children are overloaded, and their teachers too have to work very hard. Courses have to be planned in great detail. A great deal of fuss is made about marking: in every lesson, a number of children are questioned on their homework and given a grade from one (very poor — so poor that it is seldom awarded) to five (excellent), with three as a pass. Periodic assessments on this basis provide the assessment for the year, and this is used by the staff to determine whether the child should be promoted. In practice this usually happens. Reporting school and class performance on the

147

basis of pass rates led to abuses and was abolished in 1984, but it has continued here and there.

However, the Soviet school is not particularly exam-oriented. In the USSR as a whole, the important school-leaving examinations come at the end of the ninth year, as stated, and at the end of the course. Marks are also awarded for conduct, and, interestingly, pupils whose conduct marks are unsatisfactory are not allowed to sit these examinations. However, a good report from their employers will earn them the chance to do so later. Failure in one or two subjects, unless rectified by resits during the summer, means repetition of the form six course; unsuccessful form 11 pupils are given an attendance certificate only, but they have a second chance to resit the failed subjects a year later. Outstanding pupils, whose performance includes their general contribution to the life of the school, win gold medals, and those who have made excellent progress receive certificates of honour. These awards entitle future students to preferential treatment when they apply to enter higher education.

There is no systematic streaming by ability; but this does not preclude partially differentiated treatment within the class, nor a good deal of experimentation, nor, as we have seen, schools with intensive teaching in certain subjects. One should be wary of the view that the practice of keeping pupils down a year is a form of differentiation by intelligence, because streaming implies a philosophical outlook affecting the masses, whereas repeating is the fate only of a small minority (in 1982, 97.6 per cent of pupils finished the then eight-year course on time). Even so, some educationists are unhappy about making children repeat a year: this not only puts more pressure on teachers than may be good for them, but can also be bad for the pupils' morale and cause them to drop out before the end of the course. Despite sanctions on parents and exhortations to teachers, a drop-out problem does exist in the USSR. Officially, the phenomenon is considered to be exceptional, but its size cannot be gauged as no comprehensive statistics are published.

As with all Soviet institutions, the Party and its various committees exercise ultimate control of the education system and permeate it at all points, directly and indirectly. The primary Party units, which exist in every school employing at least three Party members, bear the chief responsibility, to the district committees in the first instance, for seeing that policy is put into effect. The staffs of tiny schools may be banded together to form a Party branch. The Party is the source of policy development, and the government organisations have to implement it; but implementation combined with inspection falls not only to the ministries and departments of education but also, and particularly, to the primary units. The leadership role of the school Party organisation is openly acknowledged as a 'driving force'.

MORAL EDUCATION

When we turn from the imparting of knowledge to the inculcating of values we find ourselves in territory that seems very different. The Soviet handling of moral or character education, or upbringing, is the feature of the system that rouses so much interest and hostility in the West, not that the Russians have any monopoly of political socialisation methods, but they use them to much greater purpose. This is only one way to the much-quoted goal of the all-round development of the individual, but it plays a central role, linking all the components of the educational programme: intellectual, aesthetic, physical, and polytechnical. The Pioneer detachment, identified with the school class, is of great importance here.

Soviet educationists stress two notions now, as they did fifty years ago: conscious discipline, involving a positive sense of responsibility to one's fellows, and a spirit of collectivism. These concepts have many implications. Younger pupils are sponsored by older ones, who are expected to act as mentors. Pupils are involved in the community, carrying out 'socially useful work' in their district, and local farms and factories are called upon to take an active interest in the schools. Children are exhorted to show concern for public property, not least because it is the fruit of the labours of others. They are urged to be helpful and self-reliant at home, and parents are expected to support the schools' general aims. Comradeliness is the watchword, both in the schools and in the wider world; the Soviet Union is a vast collective, and the totality of 'peace-loving peoples' of the world an even vaster one. Mutual responsibility is crystallised in pupil self-management. At a tender age, Soviet citizens are introduced to a system of government by committee and develop the habits of giving speeches, delivering reports, drafting and discussing plans, indulging in criticism and self-criticism, and

Veps children learning to read in a foreign language. The Veps language had no written form before the Revolution. (*SCR*)

disciplining offenders. All this is under the watchful eye of the adult whose role it is to guide them toward making the 'correct' decisions for themselves.

Physical education is important, partly because it requires strict discipline and can be a valuable form of collective activity, and partly because of the belief that only under Communism can people develop to physical perfection. The propaganda value is obvious: 'new Soviet people' are meant to outdo their capitalist competitors, not only on the production line but also on the Olympic track. Aesthetic education implies creativity, another of their characteristics, and there is political point in studying the achievements of great artists, especially when they are Russian or when they portray heroic figures and events. Finally, intellectual education, which involves

150

training in dialectical thinking and a materialist world view, is linked to moral education through reverence for Lenin as the great example and guide for daily living. A book for children offers this advice to young Muscovites: 'If you feel sad or worried, go to the Mausoleum and spend a few quiet moments there, with Lenin'. They are taught to sing 'Lenin is always with you' and to believe that God does not exist.

Let us sum up. Marxism-Leninism is held to be the sole repository of truth, and the Party is its unique interpreter and driving force. The school is one of the various transmission belts conveying its impulses to the masses. The goal is the transformation of society.

VOCATIONAL, TECHNICAL, AND HIGHER EDUCATION

Vocational and technical alternatives at 15-plus have already been enumerated (see also Fig. 15). Students taking the three-year courses at secondary vocational schools (*srednee professial'no-tekhnicheskoe uchilishche*, or SPTU for short) have a heavy workload, doing vocational training and general subjects in roughly equal proportions. The yearly average compulsory periods exceed those at the senior stage of general schools by about 20 per cent, while the general education component receives slightly less attention. The SPTUs are searching endlessly for ideal general-subject syllabuses. Indeed, under the February 1988 proposals, vocational schools will probably cease to award a full secondary leaving certificate. They are also fighting valiantly, and with some success, to get rid of their public image as dumping grounds for problem youngsters; this image has seriously hampered recruitment. At 17-plus, general-school leavers may enter one-year courses at technical schools. Under the 1984 reform, these are being incorporated into SPTUs. The various types of institutions in this sector between them offer training for about 1400 skilled occupations. In 1985–86, they had more than 4 million students, of whom more than 3.5 million were at day SPTUs and received some form of maintenance.

Secondary specialised schools, commonly known as technicums (though, strictly speaking, technicums are confined to industry), somewhat share the SPTUs' problem of general education because their 15-plus entrants have time only for 75 to 80 per cent of the general school hours. They do not, however, suffer from a lack of prestige. They are regarded as the next best thing to higher education; they provide courses of two years or more for 17-year-olds from general secondary schools. They have a different problem: perhaps half of their ex-students are employed in lower-level jobs than those for which they are trained. These schools give courses in more than 500 specialisms. In 1985–86, they had some 4.5 million students, including 2.9 million on a day basis, most of whom were receiving grants. Teachers are trained here and also in higher education establishments (both 'pedagogical institutes' and universities).

Higher educational institutions (*vuzy*) form the most prestigious channel of post-secondary education. In 1985–86, there were 894 of them, with more than five million students; just over half of the students were in day courses. The *vuzy* include universities (69 in 1985) but are otherwise organised by branches of the economy. Applicants must have complete secondary education and a Komsomol (Young Communist League) reference, and industrial experience helps. They have to sit competitive entrance examinations. In the early 1980s, there were said to be between two and three candidates per place, but this average for the whole USSR conceals the fact that competition is much stiffer for certain *vuzy* and in places where large numbers of the intelligentsia are clustered. Since 1969, a second chance for people who were unable to complete their secondary education has been available in special one-year courses put on by the 'preparatory departments' of *vuzy*. The majority of students receive grants; and hostel accommodation, though rather poor and cramped by British standards, is extraordinarily cheap for those who can get it. Grants were increased in 1987; how far this will reduce the need for less well-off students to take on part-time jobs remain to be seen.

Courses usually last five years and contain an obligatory component of political history and theory. With a hectic six-day week, continuous assessment, examinations twice a year, and a final-year dissertation, instruction is rigorous. Poor work can lead to the loss of one's grant, but consistently good results can cause it to be increased, as can public service. After graduation, unless exempted on compassionate grounds, one is directed for two or three years to some place where one's specialism is needed. The best students have first pick of such jobs, whereas others somehow manage never to turn up. But there is no job shortage overall.

In 1985, 61 per cent of 17-plus day general secondary-school completers continued their full-time education in various ways (a breakdown of these was not available to us) while 39 per cent went directly into jobs. For the employed, technical and higher education is provided through evening and correspondence courses. SPTU and technical-school graduates are assigned to their first posts for two years, and technicum graduates for three. But in both sectors the top 10 per cent are entitled to apply for immediate full-time admission to *vuzy*.

PROBLEMS

The essential yardstick for assessing any system of education is the extent to which it succeeds in attaining its goals. The system in the Soviet Union has made immense progress, but it still has some distance to go. The credit for rapidly transforming a relatively backward society into one of the world's two most powerful nations must be ascribed, in part, to its system of schooling. The achievements of Soviet education are reflected in the tendency of those who have experienced it to give it special praise — even including refugees and émigrés. On the other hand, reports of persistent delinquency and self-seeking attitudes filter through the Soviet press. Upbringing is still as important as ever.

An interesting question is that of the relative importance of the school and the family. Officially they are in partnership. But the primacy of the school is frequently implied. An Englishman who spent a year in a Soviet school reported that he never saw a pupil crying, but he often saw mothers in tears, presumably after a telling-off by the teacher. Parent education is part of the school's activities, and there is great concern that 'unified demands' should be made on the children. Clearly, the influence of the family remains strong. Related is the problem, familiar in our country, of differing family backgrounds creating advantages or disadvantages: Soviet sociologists have repeatedly indicated that the children of intellectuals have a better chance of entering higher education than do those of workers.

There is also the problem of equality versus special needs: needs of the state and needs of the child. They are likely to be identical in many ways because it is in the state's interest to maximise its human capital. How much education should there be, and how should it be distributed? A cardinal problem of Soviet education is one typical of mass societies — how to reconcile the goal of education for all to a high level with the goal of education of the best to the highest level. A further question is how to identify and secure the right balance between the general and vocational components of education. In particular, how far is virtual direction into vocational courses at 15-plus tolerable? In 1988, this whole problem area came back into the melting pot.

Bound up with these problems, finally, is the problem of control and conformity versus freedom and innovation. In a tightly controlled environment, where young people are taught to think along set patterns, how can there be scope for the imaginative, original thought that leading scientists deem essential for real advance? This thought, which resulted in the schools for the gifted, is a keynote of the higher education reform announced in 1986. Bureaucrats, however, tend to resist change, as recent reformers have again discovered. Meanwhile, we on the sidelines watch their efforts, certainly with fascination and perhaps with sympathy.

11

Literature and the Arts

G. S. SMITH

This discussion is confined to the literature and culture of the Russian-speaking part of the USSR. Though this culture is the dominant one in the country as a whole, it should not be forgotten that Soviet culture exists in terms of scores of languages and artistic traditions, some of which pre-date Russian culture and some of which emerged from the pre-literate stage only after 1917. Russian culture dominates partly because of the numerical ascendancy of Russian speakers and their wide geographical distribution among the nationalities whose republics constitute the USSR; partly because of the prestige of Russian cultural achievements both before and after 1917; and partly because Russian is, for historical and political reasons, the common language of the USSR, understood by educated people of all nationalities and dominating the media of communication. Officially, no contradictions are supposed to exist between the cultures of the constituent nationalities of the USSR in respect of form, so this limitation can be justified to some extent. This discussion is also largely confined to the cultural scene of recent years, which means that some of the most interesting issues about Soviet culture are not raised: for instance, the question of the extent to which it is a new phenomenon, the result of an unprecedented social and political order rather than a continuation of pre-Revolutionary tradition, and the question of the extent to which the development of Soviet culture reflects the historical phases through which the USSR has passed since 1917.

Mikhail Sholokhov, famous Soviet writer and Nobel Prize winner (*SCR*)

STATE OWNERSHIP AND
PARTY CONTROL

Immediately after the Bolsheviks took power in 1917, they instituted a system of controls over the media. This system was
completed by Stalin in the mid-1930s. It has been operated with
greater and lesser degrees of severity, giving rise to the notion of
'freeze' (very roughly speaking, 1932–41; 1946–56; 1968–81) and
'thaw' (the 1920s; the Second World War; the Khrushchev period;
and the Gorbachev period since 1985, which is continuing into
mid-1988, the time of writing). The system rests on two pillars:
ownership of the media by the State and ideological control by the

Party. The official view is that these factors liberate the artist to fulfil a responsible social function, unlike the economic and social factors that shape the arts under capitalism and deprive the artist of real freedom.

The central, inescapable fact about Soviet culture, the point from which all discussion of it must begin, is that its means of production and exchange, like all other means of production and exchange in the Soviet economy, are owned by the state with only a few exceptions. Literature and the arts form part of the planned economy of the USSR, and they compete for state resources, formulate plans, and are subject to political decisions in the same way as are other sectors of the economy. General policy decisions concerning the arts can be, and are, taken at the highest level of the Party apparatus, the Politburo. These decisions are customarily published in the leading newspapers as resolutions of the Central Committee, and, as in other spheres of Soviet life, they effectively have the status of law. The Propaganda Department of the Central Committee and the Party groups within the various organisations concerned with cultural affairs have the task of seeing that these decisions are publicised and take effect. In specific terms, the 'Party line', which is what these decisions express, is the first point of reference for those in day-to-day control of cultural affairs (such as editors of journals and the repertoire departments of theatres and film studios) in deciding what to accept, what not to accept, what to commission, and what to promote.

The political and ideological factor takes precedence over commercial and artistic considerations. The fact that a Soviet author is published in frequent and massive editions is not necessarily an indication that his or her books are being bought and read; and many books that would sell very well are not published or appear in small editions intended mainly for sale abroad. Still, the commercial factor is not negligible. Soviet authors receive royalties on their sales, and the USSR has its millionaire authors of spy stories and TV potboilers, as well as millionaire Party hacks whose work does not sell.

But it is not only broad policy decisions that are taken at the top level of the Party; there is plenty of evidence that specific cases may be decided at this level.

CONTROL BY PROFESSIONAL
ORGANISATIONS

The arts are not simply controlled by Party orders from above. The leadership seeks and acts on advice from the professional organisations. These organisations — the Unions of Writers, Composers, Artists, Architects, Journalists, and Cinematographic Workers, and the All-Union Theatrical Society — are the most effective mechanism through which to exercise control over the arts. They were introduced under Stalin in the early 1930s as part of the general effort to bring all activity in the country within the control of the Party. To a large extent, the opportunity to engage in professional artistic activity in the USSR is conditional upon membership in the appropriate organisation. They are centralised and bureaucratic. They hold Congresses every so often but, in practice, are controlled by their central secretariats; as in the case of other parallel Soviet institutions, these secretariats include a Party group that is expected to take a leading role in their activities. Although the chairmen of the professional organisations tend to be people who have made a significant contribution in their own sphere of the arts, the members of the secretariats are almost always individuals for whom a nominal contribution has provided the stepping stone to the exercise of their true bureaucratic vocation.

The Union of Writers is the most powerful and best known of the professional organisations. It is organised on a regional basis and, within its regional structure, into committees corresponding to various kinds of literature — prose, poetry, criticism, and translation. Work in progress can be submitted to these committees for discussion, and a favourable response is a useful factor in moving a work toward publication. We are fortunate enough to have a detailed account of this process at work in the rather exceptional case of Solzhenitsyn's *Cancer Ward*.

The Union of Writers also organises a system of classes and workshops for beginners. Members are expected to give their time to this work, and it forms the lowest rung of the control hierarchy.

The Union of Writers is a rich organisation. At its disposal are scarce and desirable facilities like restaurants, clubs and sanatoria, and membership is a path to a comfortable and privileged life. In consultation with the Ministry of Culture, it decides who may be permitted to travel abroad. It administers the Literary Fund (*Lit-*

Vladimir Karpov, President of the Union of Writers (*Novosti*)

fond), money accumulated from fixed-scale deductions from royalty payments and made available to members when the need arises (e.g. to support themselves when working on a project). The Union of Writers controls the most prestigious literary periodicals (*Novy mir, Oktyabr', Voprosy literatury*) and the major literary publishing house, *Sovetskii pisatel'*. These resources are much less likely to be forthcoming to unreliables, and, taken together, they constitute the most powerful set of incentives making for co-operation between writer and state. The situation is similar in the other arts.

CONTROL BY CENSORSHIP

A further fundamental instrument of control is censorship. Nothing can be published in the USSR unless it has been passed by the institution known as Glavlit (or simply Lit), the censor's office. The copy for any publication is submitted to Glavlit, whose representative goes through it and indicates what can and cannot be published. The necessary changes are made, and the revised version is resubmitted to be checked and then stamped and signed. Only with this stamp and signature will the printer accept it for reproduction in more than a few copies. The Glavlit representatives work by reference to what is colloquially known as the 'Talmud', a manual listing topics that cannot be mentioned in public print.

The Glavlit stamp and signature is by no means the first nor the last stage in the process of censorship. Before any work gets to the stage of submission to Glavlit, it must pass through the hands of many other cultural overseers. Obviously, a writer knows very well that if a work is to be published in the USSR it will eventually land on the desk of the Glavlit censor, and that writer is conditioned by this knowledge in the process of composition; this self-censorship is the most subtle and insidious element in the mesh of controls. Writers have a shrewd idea of what will pass and what probably will not, and they act accordingly. Quite likely, many writers *think* accordingly, and even that conforming has become subconscious and natural after so many years of the system's existence, just as writers in other societies are spontaneously guided by their instinct for what is commercially viable.

In the USSR, as in Russia before 1917, works of fiction normally appear in periodicals before they come out as books, and it is to the editorial board of a periodical that literary works are normally submitted in the first instance. Editorial boards contain the usual Party group whose job it is to see that the Party line is observed. Even though a determined and courageous chief editor, like Tvardovsky of *Novy Mir* during the 1960s, can exercise a liberating influence in shaping the 'profile' of the journal, the position is precarious and dependent upon political factors. A manuscript coming into the office of a journal is passed to sub-editors and readers, who make a first set of revisions in consultation with the author. Soviet writers say that the subtlest literary minds in the world are to be found in the ranks of these sub-editors; their advice is by no means always negative. Besides exercising the normal functions of cutting and stylistic supervision, sub-editors are expert in finding forms of words that will get delicate passages through without sacrificing too much of the author's thought. The sub-edited manuscript then goes before the editorial board for further discussion and, if necessary, alteration. Only then is the work set up and the copy submitted to Glavlit.

But even when all these stages have been passed and the work appears, all is not necessarily well. There is also post-publication censorship. A published work can be pounced on by critics or, even worse, singled out for adverse comment by a government spokesman. In extreme cases, this can result in the withdrawal of the work from libraries and a ban on its sale; and the author's next work will be treated with extra caution. Post-publication censorship applies most noticeably in the field of the cinema and music, where the suppression of performance is much easier than the seizure of published copies of a book or periodical. And it should not be forgotten that censorship applies not only to Soviet-produced works but also to the selection of foreign works for translation or exhibition in the USSR. Censorship applies as strictly to the past as it does to the present, so that certain phases in the history of Russian literature and art are almost unknown in their native country outside a very small circle of privileged specialists.

There are some loopholes in the system apart from the ones caused by the clumsiness of the system itself, the sheer volume of material published, and normal human fallibility. In literature, one of them arises through the use of 'Aesopian language', that is writing about forbidden subjects in terms of permitted ones. Because the Soviet reader is looking for the device, not many clues to the real subject

161

need to be planted. Another strategy is to publish outside Moscow and Leningrad, where the local Glavlit representatives may be less vigilant.

SOCIALIST REALISM, THE AUTHOR
AND THE READER

Perhaps the crucial difference between Soviet and Western censorship lies in the fact that whereas the latter is almost exclusively *proscriptive*, Soviet censorship and the controls that go with it are also *prescriptive*; the artist is told what to do as well as what not to do. What the artist should do is laid down in the general policy of the Party in the field of artistic creation, as expressed in the doctrine of Socialist Realism. There are several definitions of Socialist Realism: they range from the official — 'the truthful, historically concrete presentation of reality in its revolutionary development' combined with 'the task of the ideological remaking and education of the workers in the spirit of socialism' — to the cynical — 'Socialist Realism is praising the leaders in language they themselves can understand'. It would be futile to try to understand Socialist Realism in aesthetic terms because it is ultimately a political formula, a way of saying that the creative artist should represent life in the way the Party wants it represented at any given time, and that the ultimate loyalty of the artist is to the state rather than to art. The variety of aesthetic devices in Soviet culture at the present time is certainly too wide to be understood within the confines of realism; but although, by and large, only lip service is now paid to the aesthetic aspect of the doctrine, its political aspect has certainly not been eroded.

Apart from prescription, there is another major difference between the artistic process in the USSR and the West. In the West, what is read by the reader, seen by the viewer, and heard by the concert-goer is the result of a long series of compromises involving creative artists, producers, promoters, editors, accountants, backers, lawyers, agents, and trade unions, all of whom have their own motives and interests. But the author almost always has several alternative channels through which to reach the public and can choose the one that will interfere least with his or her purpose. The Soviet author is faced with a much more monolithic system, and artistic works in the USSR are compromises to a greater extent than

162

in the West. It is never possible to be certain how far the final product represents the author's intention, assuming, that is, that there is a final product at all, and that it has not foundered somewhere within the control system or been dismissed as unrealisable at the moment of conception. This affects the way people read and see and listen. They understand what hoops have been jumped through to get the work out, and that what is not there is probably as significant as what is. Soviet readers are, to the Western mind, almost incredibly sophisticated in this respect; they take nothing at face value and are capable of conducting debates in language that, to the non-Soviet person, is a mass of clichés and evasions, but to them is fraught with quite specific, though unmentionable, detail. And there are writers and readers sufficiently gifted to exploit this skill of their readers.

FORM AND CONTENT IN THE SOVIET ARTS

What are the wider effects of the system of control in terms of the form and content of artistic works produced in the USSR? In general, it must be said that the arts in the USSR are backward and conservative in form. One of the permanent yardsticks of Soviet criticism is whether the work in question will be comprehensible and morally beneficial to the average person. This objective, understandable and praiseworthy in a context of mass literacy only recently achieved, when institutionalised has the effect of stultifying experiment and producing a uniform middle-brow art and of preventing the existence of an *avant garde* whose experiment would revivify the mainstream. It is usually technical experimentation that Soviet critics have in mind when they reach for their favourite bogy-word, *formalism*. Many Soviet writers and artists are ashamed of the extent to which their culture has been divorced from the European and American context since the 1930s, are irked by the limitations within which they are obliged to work, and are acutely embarrassed by official proclamations about the leading role played by the USSR in the field of world culture. However, formal conservatism is by no means entirely the result of official interference; it comes also from the genuine concern of Russian intellectuals that their work should communicate, should be accessible to a wide audience rather than a privileged elite. It is worth noting that

163

Visual art of the 1920s — a
book cover designed by
S. Chekhonin, for the II
Congress of the Communist
International (1920)

'unofficial' art in Russia is not formally experimental to any large
extent. In the context of the controls described above, plain speaking
is the most daringly experimental technique possible.

In the period since the Revolution, Russia has made vital
contributions to the arts in four main areas. The first, non-
representational painting and sculpture, was largely a legacy of
pre-Revolutionary achievements. The second was in the theatre,
where Soviet directors pioneered non-realistic techniques of presentation that are still a powerful force in world drama. The third was
in the cinema, particularly in the work of Eisenstein, with his
refinement of montage, the close-up, and the crowd scene. The
fourth was in the art of the poster. All these developments took place
in the 1920s, and they were suppressed — or superseded, as the
apologists would say — in their country of origin with the rise of
Stalinism.

The effect of the control system, since it became effective in the early 1930s, has been the overwhelming predominance of variations on a few officially sanctioned themes: the vast iconography of Lenin, the heroic aspects of the last war, psychologically stable and physically robust workers and peasants building Communism, and the leading role of the Party in all aspects of life. Along with these themes go extreme prudishness in the treatment of sexual themes, and a Victorian attitude to language. In these two respects, however, as with technical experimentation, it may be that official intolerance reflects genuinely widespread assumptions about propriety in art, for it is remarkable that unofficial art also tends to avoid eroticism and low language. The most vital unofficial art form in Soviet society is the political rather than the sexual anecdote.

Does the wholesale interference with artistic creation matter in any real sense? For the majority of readers and writers it probably

'Leniniana' — a display of books by Lenin in various languages. Lenin displays are very much a feature of Soviet bookshops. (*SCR*)

165

does not. In the USSR, just as in the West, most of the people active in the arts are craftsmen doing a job in the same way as other people make shoes, clothes and furniture. They produce what they know can be sold without difficulty and provide them with a living, and they do this without cynicism or compromising their integrity. They turn out a product according to the requirements and preferences of the customer or sponsor in the West, and the Party in the USSR, and their personal fulfilment is related to the degree of professionalism in the execution of the job. It would be a difficult task to establish whether it is the demands of the customer or the Party that produce the worst art: the essential difference is that the arts are serving two different kinds of demand. And for most people, West and East, the matter is of little consequence; what they desire is escape and entertainment rather than art (which is neither), and these things can be found more easily in the spectator sports (notably ice hockey in the USSR), pulp fiction, fantasy TV, and, most easily of all, in drink.

UNOFFICIAL CULTURE

But the majority, of both consumers and producers, is not everybody, and there is another side to the story of control. The remarkable fact is that, in spite of the system of control and the concentration of resources in state hands, there are still creative artists who will not toe the line. This was true even in the worst years of Stalinism; during the 1930s and 1940s, there were men like Mandelshtam, Bulgakov and Shvarts who wrote non-conformist work with no hope of publication and with a real risk of arrest and death. The result is that the USSR has a substantial alternative tradition to the official one in the arts. People copy and disseminate officially unacceptable works of literature (*samizdat*, self-publishing) and songs on tape (*magizdat*, tape-recorder publishing). Manuscripts are sent abroad for publication (*tamizdat*, publication over there), undeterred by the International Copyright Agreement, which the Soviet Union signed in 1973 to put a stop to this process. Unpublished and suppressed works are broadcast back to the USSR (*radizdat*, radio publishing).

But technology has a major effect on the end result. Whereas works of literature can be copied, if only in relatively small numbers, paintings exist in one copy, which will remain unknown if not exhibited; the performance of music involves large numbers of people, dramatic works even more; film making requires expensive equipment and skilled labour. The spoken, written and sung word can bypass the official network to a degree unattainable by the other arts. But compared with the massive circulation figures of officially printed books and the degree of exposure available to an officially sponsored film, play, picture, or sculpture, *samizdat* and its analogues must remain a drop in the ocean, available to only a tiny proportion of the population.

Underlying the system of controls is a factor that forms the crucial difference between the situation of the arts in the USSR and the West. The situation in the USSR arises as a result of an old Russian conviction that the artistic word and image are potent forces in social and political life, forces that can be ignored by government only at its own peril. The artist must be taken seriously. In the West, intellectuals sometimes display an attitude to this situation that is tinged with masochistic jealousy. Is it preferable to be persecuted but taken seriously or to be free to speak but ignored? Perhaps artistic freedom can only be permitted when the arts have a negligible social and political effect.

RECENT DEVELOPMENTS

The treatment accorded dissident creative artists has been different at different periods of Soviet history. Under Stalin, they were imprisoned and often exterminated. During the 1960s and 1970s, they were sometimes imprisoned, but increasingly they were exiled. The result was that, by the time of Brezhnev's death in 1982, many of the most important Russian writers, musicians, painters, sculptors and dancers were living outside the USSR; within the country the arts, like the economy and social life, had been reduced to a state of sullen torpor.

Since 1985, the Party has attempted to galvanise the arts. This attempt is motivated by the Party's need to recapture credibility and even some enthusiasm on the part of the intelligentsia in order to enlist their cooperation in rebuilding the economy and social life. For the new regime of Mr Gorbachev, the arts constitute an area in

Alexander Solzhenitsyn, another Nobel Prize winner, now exiled from the Soviet Union (*Press Association*)

which quick results can be obtained for the least effort to impress both the native and the foreign observer.

Accordingly, instructions have been given to operate the control system in a more liberal way. Since 1985, certain works of literature and films that were previously banned have been permitted; almost all the works of literature concerned so far were originally created before 1965. Some works have been published that deal with previously banned topics, most notably with the Stalin period, including the collectivisation and the 'Great Terror'. There have also been calls for a restructuring (*perestroika*) of the Union of Writers. Both the Writers' Union and the Union of Cinematographers have been given a new First Secretary. Socialist Realism has been de-emphasised in Party pronouncements. Statements have been made that Glavlit no longer interferes with aesthetics, but now confines itself to preventing the publication of 'military and state

168

secrets', which was supposed to be its original task. There has also been a suggestion that members of the Union of Writers (but not writers outside the Union) should be allowed to set up private publishing co-operatives. Radical reforms have been proposed in the way films and plays are financed, in an attempt to cut through bureaucratic controls and liberate creative personnel to produce for the market. New editors have been appointed to certain journals. There have been rumours that certain exiles will be allowed to return if they wish; some of them, including Joseph Brodsky, who won the 1987 Nobel Prize for literature, have been published in Soviet journals. But the Party does not seem to have contemplated dismantling the control system itself.

The atmosphere in the arts has brightened considerably. But at the time of writing there is very little evidence of any substantial impetus coming from below to take advantage of the new relaxation that has been permitted from above. It remains to be seen whether the younger generation, alienated from the mainstream creative arts under Brezhnev and turning increasingly to rock music and its associated social phenomena, will return, among other things, to literature and produce a new generation of writers. As in other aspects of Soviet life, the seventy-year-old control system has discredited and eroded individual initiative and enterprise, and it is an enormous, but crucial, task for the Party to change this state of affairs. Whether it can do so without relinquishing its claim to unique authority is perhaps the most critical problem it faces.

12

Foreign Policy

JONATHAN HASLAM

FROM REVOLUTION TO CIVIL WAR (1917–20)

The October Revolution, which uprooted Russian society, was also a cataclysm with major international repercussions. This was due partly to the key position of Russia in world politics. Russia was a central component in the European balance of power. She was also a leading partner, alongside Britain and France, in the Entente, which was at war with Germany, Austria-Hungary and the Ottoman Empire. And it should not be forgotten that Russia was also a major power in Asia. Any significant change of regime in Russia would, therefore, have important implications for the rest of the world.

But the October revolution was not a mere change of regime. The Bolsheviks under Lenin saw themselves as one section of a world revolutionary movement. Like revolutionary France in the 1790s, the Russia of 1917 sought to transform the world in its own image, directing its appeal over the heads of the rulers into the barracks and slums of the ruled.

Such an ambitious programme was not easily realised. The revolution in Russia had been precipitated by the agonies of the First World War, and the war now threatened to engulf the revolution. The Bolsheviks were forced to sue for peace with Germany. With no army in the field, and no foreign revolution yet to the rescue, they had to accept a peace of annexations and indemnities. At Brest-Litovsk in March 1918, the Russian frontiers to the north and west were reduced to the boundaries of 1792. The revolution in Europe failed to come in time, and the Bolsheviks had to go on alone.

In this context, Soviet foreign policy acquired two aspects: support for revolution abroad; and a more traditional, hard-headed diplomacy or 'Realpolitik'. The survival of the Soviet state still

The Bolsheviks sue for peace with Germany: Kamenev, Joff, and Trotsky are met at the railway station. (*R T Hulton*)

seemed to depend ultimately upon the expansion of the revolution across the capitalist and colonial worlds. But the revolution abroad was much too slow and much too uncertain to be counted on in the short term. Compromises with the existing international order were inescapable.

These rival aspects of foreign policy were brought together within a year of the revolution in the doctrine of peaceful co-existence. On the one hand, class war would continue. Soviet Russia saw itself leader of the world working class in battle against capitalism: from 1919 to 1943, this international class war was prosecuted by the Communist International (Comintern), set up in the new capital, Moscow, on the initiative of the Russian Communist party. On the other hand, Soviet Russia as a state would seek peace with its capitalist rivals. This was the job of the People's Commissariat (later the Ministry) of Foreign Affairs. While Bolshevik diplomats pursued normal relations with foreign governments, Bolshevik agents from the Comintern attempted to secure the overthrow of these same governments. The capitalist world, naturally, did not find this an acceptable form of conduct.

171

As early as the end of December 1917, the British and French military planned a war of intervention to overthrow the revolution. In April 1918, the Japanese (with French connivance) landed in the Russian Far East; the Americans, who wanted to stop the Japanese taking too much, were in hot pursuit. In July and August, the British invaded from the north by sea and the south by land (through Iran); the French from the south by sea. The original justification for toppling the Bolsheviks was their portrayal as pro-German. With the German defeat and the end of the world war in November 1918, this justification disappeared. Nevertheless, the war of intervention was stepped up. But success eluded the interventionists. As in the wars against Revolutionary France in the 1790s, the governments of the counterrevolutionary coalition found to their horror that instead of forestalling the spread of revolution, the war was actually precipitating it. Mutinies occurred even among British troops. And foreign intervention consolidated rather than weakened the Bolshevik hold over the Russian people. As the military campaigns ran into difficulties, the Allied forces soon engaged in mutual recrimination. The Americans were the first to leave, and when the British finally pulled out in December 1919, the others were not far behind. The Japanese were the last to leave in 1922.

The experience of foreign intervention had lasting effects. It hardened the Bolshevik antipathy toward the capitalist world. It reinforced Bolshevik belief in the need to spread revolution to increase Soviet security. But it also underlined the need to develop diplomacy as a means of keeping the capitalist world divided.

THE INTERWAR YEARS (1920–41)

During the period after the intervention — from 1920 to 1927 — the Bolsheviks devoted more effort to building and training fraternal Communist Parties all over the world. At best, these Parties would lead to the hoped-for revolutions; at a minimum, they would obstruct any future mobilisation of the capitalist world against Soviet Russia. As time went by, no further revolution materialised, even in Germany. As a result of this, the tendency to use foreign Communist Parties as mere auxiliaries of Soviet foreign policy greatly increased. Soviet isolation had another important consequence. If the Soviet Union was to survive in a hostile world without being able to count on foreign revolutions, in the immediate or even more distant future the 'exploitation of inter-imperialist contradictions' by its diplomats would hardly be sufficient to guarantee Soviet security. If it was to be confident even of mere survival, Russia had to become a major industrial power at a technological level comparable to that of its likely adversaries — Britain, France, Germany and Japan.

The sharp turn toward industrialisation at the end of 1927 (see p. 36 above) came at a time of war scares involving both neighbouring Poland, then a power to be reckoned with in Eastern Europe, and Britain, then the leading power in Europe. The first five-year plan (1928–32) established the essential basis for an independent war industry and raised Soviet military power to levels surpassing those of its immediate neighbours, including both Poland and Japan. As in the 1980s under Gorbachev, the strong emphasis on economic construction was accompanied by a reduced emphasis on spreading world revolution. Stalin sought to ensure that his risky domestic economic strategy was not jeopardised by premature insurrections launched by foreign Communist Parties. He had no love for the Comintern and disliked involvement in events that developed beyond his immediate control. But revolution was in the air in the unstable capitalist world of the 1930s. Revolutionary talk continued to alarm the West, and the West invariably saw Moscow as the source of the actual or imminent social upheavals of the 1930s: the factory occupations in France in 1936, the Spanish Civil War in 1936–39, and the revolution in north-west China from 1935. In fact, there was a revolutionary process in motion across the globe quite apart from Soviet wishes and Soviet planning. It had its own dynamic only partly dependent upon Soviet behaviour, as was later clearly demonstrated by the successful and largely independent revolutions in Yugoslavia (1944–45), China (1949) and Cuba (1959–61).

In the first decade of his dictatorship (1929–39), Stalin generally neglected foreign affairs. With his attention focused on the grand design for the economic transformation of Russia, he was inevitably distracted from world politics. Neglect and ignorance, as much as miscalculation, led to the disastrous policies that opened the path to power for the Nazis in Germany in 1929–33. After Hitler took power in January 1933, the threat that this represented was at first recognised only by some people in Moscow. Later, the Soviet

173

Union led the efforts to build a coalition of powers that would hold back German expansion. But these efforts were undermined by the Western belief that the Nazi threat was greater to Russia than to themselves and by the tendency within the Soviet Union to dismiss fascist states as inherently unstable and liable to self-destruction. The strategy of collective security so vigorously advocated by Maxim Litvinov, who was People's Commissar for Foreign Affairs from 1939, and in August the German-Soviet pact established the joint and increasing scepticism at home. Litvinov was dismissed in May 1939, and in August, the German–Soviet pact established the joint dominion of the two powers over Eastern Europe and enabled Germany to fight a war in Western Europe, undisturbed by the fear of Soviet intervention.

From September 1939 to June 1940, Stalin extended the boundaries of the Soviet state to the limits of the former Russian Empire, taking over or taking back a slice of Poland (divided with Germany), a slice of Finland (after a war lasting several months), the Baltic states, and two regions of Romania (see Fig. 16). There was a clear strategic rationale for this territorial expansion. But it also testified to something more — the reassertion of old-style Imperial geopolitics.

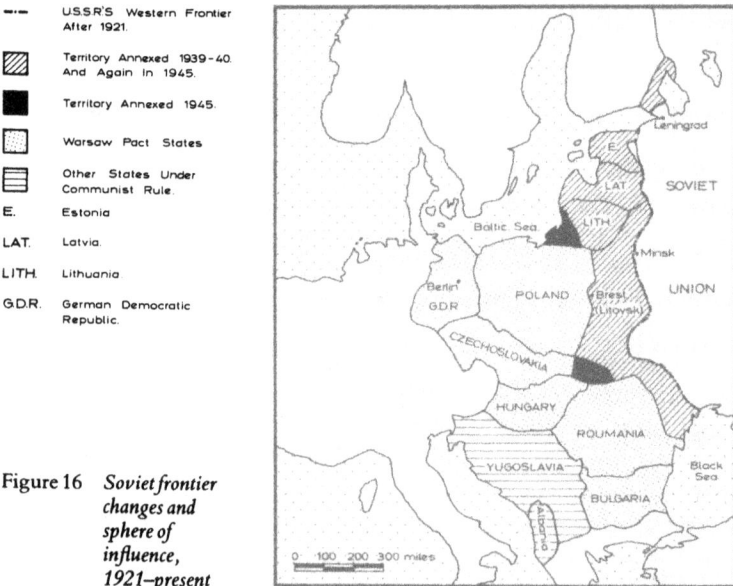

Figure 16 *Soviet frontier changes and sphere of influence, 1921–present*

Wartime devastation in a Soviet city — a street in Minsk set on fire by the retreating Germans. (*SCR*)

Russia was now a claimant to the Tsarist heritage in world politics. This was obvious in the Soviet negotiations with Japan (1940–41); the Russians refused to sign a non-aggression pact unless they recovered territory lost to Japan in the war of 1904–05. The Japanese refused to comply. (Stalin ultimately recovered the territory, and more, from Japan in 1945.)

The continuity between Tsarist Russia and the Soviet Union was reasserted at a time when the country had become materially much more powerful. But the accretion of power through industrialisation counted for nothing if the rulers were psychologically unprepared for war. In June 1941, Stalin had expected some minor conflicts on the Soviet–German border, probably followed by demands from Berlin for marginal territorial revision. But Stalin could not conceive of the full-scale German invasion that took place on 22 June 1941. He had built up Soviet power to safeguard the country from external attack and had launched the terror of 1936–39 to safeguard his own supremacy. But he now paralysed that power through his stubborn inability to recognise unpleasant reality.

THE SOVIET UNION IN THE SECOND WORLD WAR (1941–45)

Between June 1941 and May 1945, the Soviet Union was engaged in a devastating war in which vast areas of Soviet territory were occupied by a savage invader, and most of the industry built up in the 1930s was destroyed. Some 20 million Soviet lives were lost. At the outset of the German invasion, Stalin naturally feared that Britain, having fought alone in 1940–41, in the face of Soviet indifference, might seek peace with Germany, leaving the Soviet people to fight on alone. Despite the misgivings of some leading British politicians, Churchill's government declared for an Anglo–Soviet alliance. Britain was now relieved of German pressure; the air raids stopped shortly before June 1941 and were not resumed until the rocket attacks of 1944. German might, backed by the resources of occupied Europe, was directed almost exclusively to the East. The Russians, in fact, had to bear the brunt of German forces entirely alone. For a time during the desperate attempt to hold the line at Stalingrad in August–November 1942, the Russian front was in danger of collapsing (see Fig. 17). In spite of these adverse conditions, Stalin was unable to secure British and American recognition of the

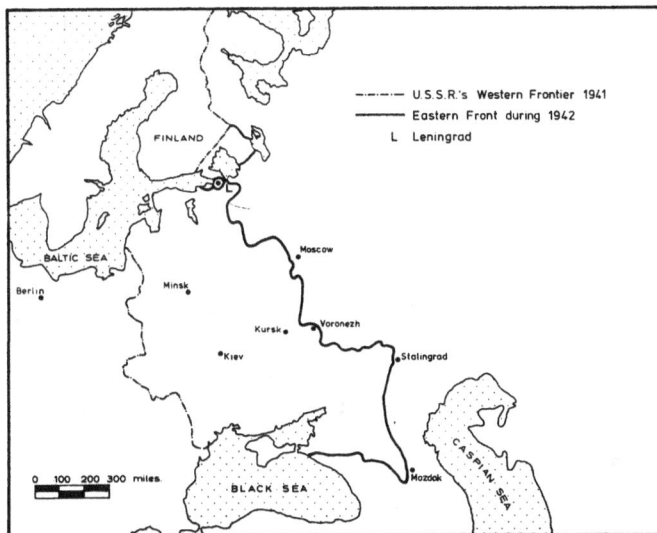

Figure 17   *German invasion of the USSR: the German eastern front in 1942*

expanded Soviet frontiers, and Allied aid was not at first forthcoming in any quantity. With a bitter sense of grievance and isolation, Stalin fell prey to the suspicion that Britain was contemplating a separate peace with the Germans. The irony was that aid from the allies became available in abundance only after 1942, when Soviet thinking about the postwar world was no longer in flux. Stalin had already decided that the Soviet Union must act on its own to solve its security problems. Allied aid was used not merely to drive back the Germans but also to take over Eastern Europe and build an iron curtain against the world outside.

In this complex mesh of circumstances, we find the origins of the Cold War. It undoubtedly suited Stalin's nature to act on his own — to choose a unilateral rather than a multilateral solution to the Soviet security problem. Personality thus played its part. But the decision that the only socialist state must rely on its own strength also harmonised with the Marxist–Leninist emphasis on what divided East from West rather than what they had in common. It is also true that the unilateral solution in no way precluded the expansion of the revolution; the Red Army carried Communist power onto occupied soil. But the behaviour of the West itself also played a role. In 1933–39, it had refused to cooperate with the Soviet Union to

177

forestall German and Japanese expansion; Litvinov's pursuit of a multilateral security system failed largely through Western failure to cooperate. And then, in the desperate days of 1941–42, the multilateral cooperation in time of war contributed little to the Soviet war effort.

THE COLD WAR (1945–53)

The tension at the end of the Second World War between the USSR and her former allies developed into the Cold War in the years that followed. The devastation wrought by war had left Europe in disarray. The end of the war reopened the prospect of revolution in the West on any scale for the first time since the end of the First World War. The role of Communists in the resistance movements and their continuing close association with the victors of Stalingrad gave them unprecedented popularity. Moreover, the defeat of the German armies of occupation and their puppet governments effectively discredited the Right throughout Western Europe. Hopes ran high for the new and better world that would follow the disillusionment of the economic crisis of the 1930s and the horrors of Nazi occupation; but, in the economic dislocation that followed, disillusion soon set in, and the people were open to revolutionary agitation. In these conditions, and with the United States backing out of Europe as it had done in 1918–19, West European leaders looked nervously at the presence of the Red Army next door in Eastern Europe. The balance of power had shifted decisively to Soviet advantage, not merely because the Red Army stood in Berlin but also because the entire continent was drifting of its own volition, apparently irrevocably, into the Communist camp.

In such conditions, West European leaders called on the New World to redress the balance of the Old. The means by which this was done was quite simply to scare the United States with the spectre of Communism, with the threat that if Europe fell, the Americas would follow.

Soviet policy made this inevitable. This was not because Stalin fostered revolution in Western Europe. On the contrary, in 1943, he abolished the Comintern and, in 1946, advised against the Communists taking up arms in Greece. Soviet leaders brusquely dismissed proposals from diehards within the Italian Communist Party

178

Stalin as international statesman. Here he is presented by Churchill with the sword of state, a gift to the people of Stalingrad (Tehran, November 1943). (*SCR*)

which carried with them the prospect of civil war. Rather, it was the insensitivity displayed by Stalin asserting Soviet control over Eastern Europe and the excessive Soviet demands upon the West that alerted the former USSR allies to the unpleasant and irreversible consequences of risking any form of subjection to Soviet power. And West European Communist Parties, mobilised into action with the formation of the Communist Information Bureau (Cominform) in 1947, gave no indication that the form of socialism they envisaged would in practice be anything different from that established by widespread repression throughout Eastern Europe.

Why was Soviet policy so inept? This subject has yet to be researched. But apparently the Soviet leaders gravely under-estimated the United States. The predominant opinion in Moscow, even as late as 1949, was that the U.S. economy would suffer a crash after the wartime boom. Whether Stalin entirely held to this belief is

179

open to doubt; his Foreign Minister Molotov certainly did. It is true that Stalin moved decisively to acquire the atomic bomb, thereby acknowledging the potential immensity of American power (see Ch. 13), but he consistently underrated American resolve. This fundamental miscalculation led to some reckless moves, including the initial refusal to remove Soviet troops from northern Iran (1946), the imposition of a blockade of West Berlin (1948), and Soviet complicity in the North Korean invasion of South Korea (1950). All these moves were intended to advance Soviet pieces across the world chessboard, with a view to future conflict with Germany and Japan, and were therefore rational in terms of geopolitical positioning. But they had a crucial impact in hardening U.S. resolve. This ultimately worsened Soviet security. By 1953, the USSR was surrounded by a ring of American air bases. A nuclear arms race was under way between Moscow and Washington. In this race, the pre-eminence of U.S. technology ensured that the Soviet Union could not win.

FROM COLD WAR TO DETENTE (1953–64)

Although the death of Stalin in 1953 opened the way for new thinking, a legacy of deep mistrust remained between East and West. In part this was inevitable because the world outside Europe and the United States was still in the throes of revolutionary upheaval. Empires were collapsing as colonialism lost its grip in the face of guerrilla insurrection. However sceptical Stalin had been of foreign revolutions, he was impelled to take advantage of them as a means of displacing the Western Powers from the greater part of the globe. But the tension in Europe and the progress of the arms race were another matter entirely.

After Stalin's death dramatic changes occurred. In 1953, the Korean war was quickly brought to an end. In 1954, a provisional settlement was reached in warring Indochina. In 1955, troops were withdrawn from a neutralised Austria. In 1955–56, an attempt was made to reach a peace settlement with Japan. Relations with other Communist powers were also restructured. Yugoslavia had been expelled from the Communist camp for disobedience in 1948, but the new Soviet leaders unsuccessfully tried to persuade it to re-enter the Communist fold. Relations with Communist China were also established on more egalitarian terms. The new Soviet leadership under Malenkov (1953–55) also reasserted the principles of peaceful co–existence and announced that war between the two camps was no longer inevitable. While more actively seeking agreement with the West, the USSR simultaneously endeavoured to undermine Western global predominance through courting the emerging and hitherto neglected Third World. In this respect the death of Stalin meant a return to Leninism, though in many other respects, the elements of continuity were more evident than were the forces of change.

This period of transition was by no means smooth. Khrushchev supplanted Malenkov in 1955 and publicly denounced Stalin in the following year (see Ch. 5). This dramatic act not only forced a reluctant regime to confront a brutal and unhappy past but also removed the ultimate symbol of authority from what had been, up to now, a highly centralised world Communist movement. West European Communist parties were badly shaken and some irreparably damaged by the new revelations. In Eastern Europe, unrest swelled into rebellion, and in 1956 the uprising in Hungary was

The Soviet Union meets the Third World — Khrushchev and Brezhnev greet the King of Afghanistan (deposed 1974). (*SCR*)

suppressed only through force from outside. Relations with the Chinese also deteriorated as a result of Khrushchev's denunciation of Stalin. And, with the Communist camp in disarray, Soviet confidence in negotiating with the West was critically undermined. Thereafter under Khrushchev, Soviet foreign policy lurched between two extremes — from threats to summitry, from the reckless installation of missiles in Cuba in 1962 to the Partial Ban on nuclear tests in 1963.

This chronic inconsistency certainly fitted Khrushchev's erratic personality; it reflected his ignorance of the external world and was exacerbated by his open contempt for specialists. But it also resulted from other factors. The Western Powers were uncertain and often divided about how to deal with the Russians. Khrushchev was under pressure to employ Soviet power in opposition to the West, both from his rivals at home and from China, the chief Soviet ally. But despite the Soviet propaganda victory when the first *sputnik* was launched in 1957, the United States was much more powerful than the Soviet Union militarily as well as economically. Khrushchev had to negotiate from weakness. His humiliating withdrawal of missiles from Cuba under threat from the United States demonstrated that the Russians had to attain strategic parity before they could seriously come to terms with the West. Not surprisingly, this became the major objective of the Soviet regime under Kosygin and Brezhnev after Khrushchev was ousted in 1964 (see Ch. 5).

DETENTE AND AFTER (1964–85)

In 1964–68, Chairman of the Council of Ministers Alexei Kosygin appeared to be the dominant figure in foreign policy. His influence soon waned, however. Leonid Brezhnev, the Party General Secretary, supplanted him by the end of the decade. But, under both Kosygin and Brezhnev, decision making was collective rather than individual. This gave foreign policy a new consistency, the result of a carefully crafted consensus, drawing on the specialists, including Foreign Minister Andrei Gromyko, who had so long been disregarded by Khrushchev. An asset at first, this form of consensus politics later became an enormous obstacle to change when new conditions urgently demanded new policies.

The focus from 1964 was, at first, on defence rather than on foreign policy: strategic rearmament as a prelude to negotiation with the United States and conventional rearmament to ensure recognition of the finality of the postwar division of Europe. It is true that diplomacy played an important role in forestalling the acquisition of nuclear weapons by West Germany (the Non-Proliferation Treaty of 1968). But elsewhere diplomacy failed, and the iron fist emerged from the velvet glove. In 1968, relations with the Dubček reformist regime in neighbouring Czechoslovakia broke down; Soviet and allied forces intervened to restore their version of order. By 1969, relations with China, already tense under Khrushchev, deteriorated to the point at which Soviet and Chinese forces were embattled on the Sino–Soviet frontier. The Vietnam war greatly worsened relations with the United States. The United States poured troops into South Vietnam to buttress a regime under attack from Communist guerrillas backed by the Communist North and, in 1965, began to bomb the North Vietnamese capital. This led the Soviet Union to break with the practice of the Khrushchev period by renewing support for revolutionaries in Vietnam and later elsewhere in the Third World.

In the early 1970s, these policies secured notable successes. In Europe, the invasion of Czechoslovakia in 1968 finally tipped the scales in West Germany toward recognition of the realities of postwar Europe (1970), and the other Western Powers duly followed suit (Helsinki Final Act, 1975). In 1972, Soviet rearmament drew the United States into the compromise SALT I agreement limiting strategic nuclear arms (see Ch. 13). In 1974–75, the Communist cause triumphed in South Vietnam, and the United States suffered a staggering blow to its prestige. Thus the new toughness in Soviet foreign policy, combined with limited negotiating flexibility, appeared to be reaping a substantial harvest. The Soviet leaders saw no reason why the U.S. decline should not continue indefinitely. A new revolutionary wave was engulfing the Third World, not just in Vietnam but also in places as far removed as Portugal and its colonies Angola and Mozambique, and in Afghanistan, Ethiopia and Nicaragua. It seemed not only ideologically correct but also politically opportune to further the spread of revolution across the globe from Moscow. And the success of SALT seemed to demonstrate that nuclear rearmament was not an obstacle to East-West negotiations but a necessary precondition and incentive.

183

The combination of Marxist–Leninist revolutions in the Third World and continuing Soviet rearmament was accompanied by excessive boasting about the shift in the correlation of world forces to Soviet advantage. This alarmed not only the Right in the United States but also the Social Democratic Left, which was dominant in Europe. From 1977, anti-Soviet sentiment mounted in both Western Europe and the United States, and by 1979, when the United States and USSR signed the second SALT treaty, detente was seriously in jeopardy. SALT II was never ratified by the United States, and by the end of 1979 the European members of NATO were committed to place U.S. Cruise and Pershing II missiles on their soil targeted against the Soviet Union (see Ch. 13). By this time, Soviet suspicions of U.S. intentions were equally strong. Faced with the prospect of the collapse of a Marxist–Leninist regime in neighbouring Afghanistan and the spectre of U.S. influence dominating in its place, the Russians made the fateful decision to invade Afghanistan and install a government on which they could rely. This accelerated the downfall of detente. By 1981, the Soviet Union faced a new administration in Washington, headed by President Ronald Reagan, which was dedicated to reviving United States power and to rolling back Soviet influence in the world.

Accustomed only to success, the ageing Brezhnev regime was slow to react. The only new departure was the opening of some negotiations to patch up differences with China (1982). It was more comfortable to cling to the assumption that the correlation of forces could not easily be reversed than to reconsider the policies that had apparently yielded so much in the past. Since 1976, matters had been made worse by the decline in the rate of growth of the economy, which made it necessary to redistribute resources from defence to other economic sectors. This caused dissent within the armed forces and made any policy, other than one of firm resistance to pressure from the United States, difficult to sustain.

In 1982, Brezhnev's death briefly opened up the possibility of breaking the mould when Yuri Andropov became General Secretary. But Andropov was soon incapacitated by ill-health and died in 1984 (see Ch. 5), to be succeeded by the ineffective and ailing Chernenko (see Ch. 5). In spite of the general immobility of Chernenko's regime, his government, under the growing influence of his second-in-command Mikhail Gorbachev, initiated talks with the United States. By this time, the Soviet Union had little choice but to confront the bitter consequences of having delayed decisive action to resolve the problems that had been accumulating over the previous decade. After Chernenko's death in early 1985, these considerations undoubtedly played a major role in the choice of Gorbachev as the new General Secretary.

THE NEW CHALLENGE TO THE WEST (1985–)

By the early 1980s, the Soviet Union faced the prospect of an arms race on a new technological level (see Ch. 13). But Gorbachev recognised that the Soviet Union had to make economic reconstruction the top priority and that this would require the transfer of resources from the military to the civilian sector. The Soviet Union could not afford a new arms race; the response to the challenge posed by the SDI (Strategic Defense Initiative or Star Wars), announced by Reagan in 1983, therefore had to be diplomatic rather than military.

The new emphasis on diplomacy as against defence highlighted the inadequacies of Gromyko's tenure as Foreign Minister. Under Gromyko and Brezhnev, Soviet foreign policy had centred almost entirely on its relations with the United States. In pursuit of detente with the United States and in search of acceptance of the Soviet Union as an equal by the Americans, the Russians paid insufficient attention to the interests of Western Europe and of Japan, the rising power in the East. In his first year of office, Gorbachev removed Gromyko and replaced him with the more pliable Eduard Shevardnadze; in the following year, he brought the experienced and pragmatic ambassador, Anatoly Dobrynin, home from Washington to head the Party Central Committee International Department. Gorbachev took the decisive step of redefining security as a political rather than a military matter and embarked on a policy of appeasing all the major powers, not just the United States, as a means of lessening East–West tension and, ultimately, of forestalling implementation of the SDI.

In the process, Gorbachev was willing to sacrifice strategic advantage for gains in political influence, taking one step back militarily in order to take two steps forward politically. No aspect of foreign policy was closed to reconsideration, whether with respect to Western Europe, Israel, China, or Japan. In seeking to extend Soviet influence over the Third World, the emphasis shifted from

Mikhail Gorbachev meets Margaret Thatcher in Moscow, April 1987. (*Novosti*)

support for revolutionary movements to the improvement of relations with existing governments. This made sense both because the revolutionary impetus of the 1970s had spent itself and because Soviet involvement in revolutionary activities had played a decisive role in the breakdown of detente with the West.

In these respects, the changes in Soviet foreign policy inaugurated by Gorbachev have been purely tactical. They are changes Lenin himself would have recognised and certainly not condemned. Over more than half a century, Soviet foreign policy has fluctuated between periods of blatant involvement in spreading revolution abroad and periods of retrenchment, between periods of military assertiveness and periods of military restraint. The factors at work include the ebb and flow of the world revolutionary process, the relative economic vitality of East and West, and the balance of military power between the two camps. The changes initiated by Gorbachev do not necessarily signal an end to ideological rivalry between East and West. Rather, they represent a bold attempt to remove that rivalry from the military to the political arena. In this

186

sense, Gorbachev's foreign policy throws down a new challenge to the West. Whether or not this policy can be sustained against domestic opposition within the USSR is still an open question; whether the West can respond as deftly as the challenge is delivered is also uncertain. But an end to the East–West struggle is certainly not yet in sight.

13

The Soviet Future in a Nuclear Age

DAVID HOLLOWAY

On 24 July 1945, President Truman approached Stalin after one of the formal sessions in Potsdam, where the leaders of Britain, the United States and the Soviet Union were meeting to decide on a postwar settlement, and casually mentioned to him that 'We have a new weapon of unusual destructive force'. Stalin nodded his head but made no reply. Truman and Churchill (who was watching intently from nearby) were convinced that Stalin had not grasped that Truman was referring to the atomic bomb. But they were mistaken, for Stalin knew of the Anglo–American effort to build the bomb and had already initiated a Soviet project in 1942. Less than a month later, after the American bombing of Hiroshima and Nagasaki, Stalin converted the small Soviet project into an all–out effort to build a Soviet bomb as quickly as possible.

The brief exchange at Potsdam marked the emergence of the atomic bomb as an overt factor in East–West relations, and the destruction of Hiroshima two weeks later demonstrated to the world the immense power of the new weapon. Since then, the Soviet Union, like other states, has been confronted by profoundly important questions about war, diplomacy, and the meaning of history. Would a nuclear war mean the end of world civilisation? Can nuclear war be prevented in an international system in which war is endemic? Can nuclear weapons be used as instruments of foreign policy? Do nuclear weapons have a military utility?

STALIN AND THE BOMB (1945–53)

In 1945, when Stalin decided to build the atomic bomb, the Soviet Union had just won a bitter and destructive war against Germany, and this victory had greatly enhanced the Soviet position in world politics. In spite of the terrible hardships the Soviet people had suffered, Stalin decided that the country needed to build up its military–industrial and military–technological might to guard, he said, against 'all contingencies'. In the second half of 1945 and the first half of 1946, he launched programmes to develop not only the atomic bomb but also ballistic and cruise missiles, radar, and jet aircraft.

These decisions were rooted in an autarchic, unilateral conception of security. Stalin believed that Soviet security would have to depend on Soviet efforts rather than on cooperation with other states. He did not anticipate war with the West in the near future, but he was afraid that peace between the major powers might last no longer than the 20 years between the two World Wars. Therefore he decided that the Soviet Union needed to master the new military technologies that other countries had developed during the war. Stalin also feared that the atomic bomb had upset the new balance of power created by the defeat of Germany and that the United States would be able to pursue a policy of atomic diplomacy, using the atomic bomb to force the Soviet Union to make political concessions. He therefore adopted a dual policy: to deprive the United States of any possible political advantage from its atomic monopoly, and to build a Soviet bomb as quickly as possible.

Both elements of Stalin's policy were successful. Stalin tried to lessen the American ability to exploit the bomb for political purposes by playing down the significance of the new weapon. 'Atomic bombs', he told a Western journalist in 1946, 'are meant to frighten those with weak nerves'; and he was determined to show that the Russians did not have weak nerves. The Soviet Union destroyed the American atomic monopoly with the first Soviet nuclear test in August 1949; this was earlier than the Americans had expected and spurred them to develop the hydrogen bomb. By 1950, the Soviet Union was also working flat out on this weapon, and both countries tested thermonuclear bombs in the early 1950s.

Until the mid-1950s, however, the Soviet Union was unable to deliver weapons against the United States, whereas American

189

bombers could strike the Soviet Union from bases in Europe and other sites near the Soviet borders. The United States thus retained a clear nuclear superiority throughout this period; but it did not gain any major political advantage from this superiority. On only two occasions before the mid-1950s can it be argued that American nuclear threats affected Soviet policy: during the Soviet blockade of West Berlin in 1948, when the movement of American bombers to Western Europe may have dissuaded Stalin from trying to stop the Western airlift; and in 1953, when the American threat to use nuclear weapons may have helped to end the Korean War. But even in these two instances the evidence is ambiguous, for it is difficult to disentangle the effect of the nuclear threat from the influence of other factors.

KHRUSHCHEV AND MISSILE
DIPLOMACY (1953–64)

During the ten years after Stalin's death the Soviet Union acquired nuclear forces capable of striking the United States. In 1956, the first Soviet intercontinental bomber entered service, and two years later the Soviet Union tested the world's first intercontinental ballistic missile (ICBM). Soviet intercontinental nuclear forces remained inferior to those of the United States, however, and in the early 1960s an American first strike could have destroyed most of the Soviet forces. In retaliation, the Soviet Union could have devastated Western Europe, but Soviet leaders may not have been sure that the threat to do this would deter the United States under all circumstances.

The years of Khrushchev's rule were a period of upheaval in Soviet defence policy. Stalin had allowed little discussion of the implications of nuclear weapons. With the development of the hydrogen or thermonuclear bomb, however, this question could no longer be ignored, because these weapons are very much more powerful than the atomic bomb dropped on Hiroshima. (In 1961, the Soviet Union tested a bomb with an explosive yield of 58 megatons, almost 3000 times more powerful than the Hiroshima bomb and equivalent to 17 times all the bombs dropped during World War II.) When Khrushchev became First Secretary of the Party Central Committee in September 1953 (only weeks after the first

The new, highly capable MIG-29/FULCRUM air defence interceptor. (*U.S. Embassy*)

Soviet hydrogen bomb test), he was briefed about nuclear weapons and, he later said, could not sleep for several days afterwards. In March 1954, Malenkov, then Chairman of the Council of Ministers, declared that world war in the nuclear age would mean the 'destruction of world civilization'. This view, which implied that it would be impossible to win a nuclear world war, was not acceptable to the leadership as a whole.

In 1956, Khrushchev introduced a new element into Soviet thinking when he declared that the growing might of the Soviet Union and its allies made war no longer 'fatalistically inevitable'. This has remained a basic premise of Soviet policy. This new position did not exclude the possibility of a world war between imperialism and socialism. The Soviet Union therefore had to prepare for war, to assess what such a war might be like, and determine what forces might be needed to wage it.

In January 1960, after much discussion within the armed forces, Khrushchev unveiled a new military doctrine. A third world war, he said, would be a war of unprecedented destruction because it would be a war between social systems in which thermonuclear weapons would be used. Such a war would begin with nuclear missile strikes deep into the enemy interior, and it would end with the victory of

Summitry in 1959: Khrushchev presents U.S. President Dwight D. Eisenhower with a replica of the pennant delivered by Soviet rocket to the moon. Vice-President Richard M. Nixon looks on. (*SCR*)

socialism because people would understand that 'capitalism is the source that breeds war and [would] no longer tolerate that system, which brings sufferings and disasters to mankind'.

Khrushchev may have thought that this was a satisfactory basis for victory, but it is evident that the High Command did not. In a book published in 1962, Marshal V. D. Sokolovskii, a former Chief of the General Staff, argued that 'victory in a future war will not come by itself. It must be thoroughly prepared and provided for'. He felt that the Soviet Union should aim for superiority over potential enemies and acquire strategic nuclear forces that could destroy the enemy's strategic forces and economic potential. Sokolovskii hinted at the importance of striking first if war could not be avoided.

Khrushchev relied very heavily on nuclear weapons in his defence policy. He believed that conventional weapons, such as tanks, manned aircraft and surface warships, had been made obsolete. He cut the armed forces by 2 million men in the mid-1950s and proposed another cut of more than 1 million in 1960. He argued, against the views of many military men, that the military power of the state was defined not by the number of men under arms but by the firepower of nuclear weapons. His relations with the High Command, like his relations with other powerful groups in the Soviet state, were marked by conflict and disagreement.

192

The nuclear emphasis in Khrushchev's policy was also reflected in his foreign policy. He believed that the fear of nuclear war could be exploited for political ends. He once told President Nasser of Egypt that 'the people with the strongest nerves will be the winners. This is the most important consideration in the power struggle of our time. The people with weak nerves will go to the wall'. From the Suez crisis of 1956 to the Cuban missile crisis of 1962 he rattled his missiles in an effort to intimidate the Western powers into making political concessions. His policy helped to precipitate two of the most dangerous crises of the nuclear age — the Berlin crisis of 1961 and the Cuban missile crisis of 1962 — but it did not achieve the results he desired.

Khrushchev was well aware of the destructive potential of nuclear weapons; for this reason he regarded them as powerful instruments of diplomacy. But the recognition that nuclear war would be immensely destructive also constrained him, for he was careful not to threaten the use of nuclear weapons when there was a serious chance that he might have to carry out his threat.

BREZHNEV AND STRATEGIC PARITY
(1964–82)

When Khrushchev was removed from office in October 1964, the United States had four times as many intercontinental strategic forces — ICBMs, submarine-launched ballistic missiles (SLBMs), and heavy bombers — as the Soviet Union. There were those in Washington who believed that the Soviet Union had now dropped out of the arms race. But that judgement proved mistaken; over the next ten years the Soviet Union made a determined effort to catch up with the United States. In 1965 or 1966, it began to deploy a new generation of ICBMs, which gave it an assured retaliatory capability. With the rapid deployment of these ICBMs and of new SLBMs, the Soviet Union began to attain parity; by 1972, it had the same number of delivery vehicles as the United States (about 2140). By then, however, the United States had begun to deploy multiple warheads on its missiles, and it therefore had more warheads than the Soviet Union. In 1975, the Soviet Union in its turn began to deploy multiple warheads on a new generation of ICBMs.

Strategic parity has two related meanings: first, the two sides have

The mobile SS-21, an improved short-range nuclear missile available to Soviet divisions opposite NATO. (*U.S. Embassy*)

approximately the same number of launchers and warheads; second, and more important, each side has the capacity to retaliate in a devastating way, even if attacked first. The attainment of strategic parity with the United States was described in the 1986 Programme of the Soviet Communist Party as an achievement of historic significance. The Soviet Union had now caught up with the United States in a key element of power, and it expected significant political advantages to follow from this new relationship.

Strategic parity opened the way to arms control. Talks on the international control of atomic energy had begun in 1946 but had proved fruitless. It was only after the Cuban Missile Crisis, which had brought the world to the brink of nuclear war, that the Soviet Union and the United States signed the Partial Test-Ban Treaty (along with Britain), which prohibited nuclear tests except those conducted underground, and the Hot Line Agreement, which made possible rapid communication in time of crisis. In 1969, the two super powers began the Strategic Arms Limitation Treaty (SALT) talks, which resulted in the Anti-Ballistic Missile (ABM) Treaty and the Interim Agreement on Offensive Missiles, which Brezhnev and Nixon signed during the Moscow summit of 1972. The ABM Treaty set limits to deployment of defences against ballistic missiles. The Interim Agreement set limits on the number of offensive missile launchers that the two sides could deploy, but it did not restrain the number of warheads that they carried.

In signing the ABM Treaty, the Soviet Union and the United States recognised that the deployment of strategic defences by one side would merely encourage the other side to expand its offensive forces; therefore, strategic defences had to be limited if there was to be any hope of limiting offensive forces. But it proved extremely difficult to build on the foundation laid in 1972. The number of strategic warheads on either side grew rapidly as both countries deployed multiple warheads, and progress toward a second SALT Treaty was slow. The Soviet Union wanted to limit cruise missiles, but the United States was unwilling to do so. Fearing that all U.S. ICBM sites would be destroyed in a first strike, the United States pressed the Soviet Union to reduce its force of more than 300 heavy ICBMs, but without success. It was not until 1979 that the SALT II Treaty was signed, after each side recognised that it could not force unwanted reductions on the other.

The relationship has remained one of strategic parity, in both meanings of the term, since the early 1970s. Soviet leaders believed that strategic parity was a major factor in the growth of Soviet power. They argued that the correlation of forces was moving in their favour and were convinced that this provided the basis for detente, because it compelled the West, especially the United States, to adopt a more accommodating attitude to Soviet interests. But in the second half of the 1970s Soviet–American detente came under increasing strain and collapsed after the Soviet invasion of Afghanistan in December 1979. This reaction showed that the basic premise underlying Soviet detente policy had been wrong. Far from making the West more accommodating, the build-up of Soviet military forces had ultimately provoked a reaction. The Reagan administration took office in 1981 with the intention of building up American military power. When Brezhnev died in November 1982, East–West relations had entered a tense and confrontational period.

THE NATURE OF SOVIET
MILITARY DOCTRINE

The interpretation of Soviet military doctrine became a highly controversial issue in the West in the late 1970s. Opponents of arms

KIROV-class, nuclear-powered, guided-missile cruiser. (*U.S. Embassy*)

control and detente argued that military publications like the Sokolovskii volume showed that the Soviet leaders did not accept mutual deterrence and were preparing to fight and win a nuclear war. They pointed to various aspects of Soviet policy, for example the large civil defence programme and the heavy ICBMs, as indications that the Soviet and American attitudes toward nuclear war were different; the Soviet Union was willing to withstand a much larger number of casualties than was the United States. The Soviet Union, the argument ran, knew how to derive important military and political advantages from its strategic forces.

These critics argued that the Soviet Union had signed the ABM Treaty not because it accepted the relationship of mutual deterrence, but because it was afraid that an American ABM system would prevent Soviet missiles from destroying American strategic forces in a first strike. They argued that arms control was a snare and a delusion for the West because it lowered people's vigilance, and dismissed as propaganda Brezhnev's statements, which he began to make in 1977, that parity, not superiority, was the goal of Soviet policy.

This argument had serious implications for policy; it suggested that the United States needed to be able to fight and win a nuclear war to deter a Soviet attack and that the United States should

196

therefore seek superiority. This view became very influential in the United States and coloured the thinking of the Reagan administration. It was criticised by Soviet leaders as a misrepresentation of their attitude to nuclear war. When President Reagan said in 1981 that 'the Soviet Union has made it very plain among themselves they believe [a nuclear war] is winnable', Brezhnev replied by stating that 'to try to outstrip each other in the arms race or to expect to win a nuclear war is dangerous madness'.

In fact, Soviet military doctrine does seem to have changed as the Soviet Union attained parity with the United States. In the 1950s and 1960s, nuclear weapons were regarded as a means of increasing the firepower available to the armed forces. In the 1970s and 1980s, however, the rapid growth in the number of nuclear weapons and delivery vehicles led, in the words of Marshal N. V. Ogarkov, who was Chief of the General Staff from 1977 to 1984, 'to a radical review of the role of these weapons, to a break with previous views of their place and significance in war, of the methods of conducting battles or operations, and even of the possibility of waging war at all with the use of nuclear weapons'.

The recognition that nuclear war would be catastrophic — that in some real sense it could not be waged — was accompanied by greater attention to the possibility that a conflict between the Warsaw Pact and North Atlantic Treaty Organisation (NATO) in Europe might be confined to conventional (non-nuclear) weapons. Changes in the organisation of Soviet forces in the late 1970s and early 1980s seemed to indicate that the Soviet Union was seriously interested in the 'conventional option' and that it believed that, even in the event of a major conflict in Europe, it might be able to deter NATO from resorting to nuclear weapons. The Soviet pledge not to be the first to use nuclear weapons, made at the United Nations in 1982, seems to fit into this pattern of Soviet thinking about nuclear weapons.

In this context, it seems plausible that the Soviet Union signed the ABM Treaty out of fear of a costly technological race from which it might emerge worse off and not merely because it wanted to be able to launch a first strike at U.S. ICBM silos without hindrance. In any event, when President Reagan made his Star Wars (Strategic Defense Initiative) speech in March 1983, calling for a complete defence against nuclear missiles, the Soviet Union reacted with dismay and interpreted the Strategic Defense Initiative (SDI) as part of an American drive to regain strategic superiority.

GORBACHEV AND THE 'NEW THINKING' (1985–   )

Under the heading of 'new thinking', Gorbachev has elaborated a concept of security that redefines the role of nuclear weapons and military power in Soviet policy. Gorbachev has said more clearly than any other Soviet leader that victory in a nuclear war is impossible. The basic question of security, therefore, is not whether nuclear forces can be deployed that will defeat the enemy, but whether nuclear war can be prevented so that the human race will survive. The 'new thinking' has rejected the view that the Soviet Union should prepare to fight and win a nuclear war to ensure the triumph of socialism over capitalism. The mission of socialism is to save humanity from destroying itself.

Gorbachev has also argued that security is becoming increasingly a political matter that cannot be ensured by military means alone. A country cannot make itself more secure just by building up its military forces. As Gorbachev put it, 'The character of present-day weaponry leaves no country with any hope of safeguarding itself solely with military–technical means, for example, by building up a defence, even the most powerful'. In this context, he has argued that security in the Soviet–American relationship can only be mutual: neither side can feel secure if the other feels insecure.

Summit meeting between Mikhail Gorbachev and American President Ronald Reagan in Reykjavik, Iceland, October 1986. (*Novosti*)

In January 1986, Gorbachev called for the elimination of all nuclear weapons by the year 2000. He has taken numerous initiatives in arms control negotiations and reversed many earlier policy positions. In 1987, for example, he and Reagan signed an Intermediate-Range Nuclear Forces (INF) Treaty that embodied an American proposal the Soviet Union had rejected for years; for the first time, Americans would be allowed to inspect Soviet installations. He continues to seek an agreement with the United States that would reduce strategic offensive forces while constraining the Strategic Defense Initiative.

Gorbachev has called for conventional arms reductions in Europe and has urged NATO and the Warsaw Pact to adopt force postures that are purely defensive and not threatening to the other side. If Gorbachev is willing to reduce Warsaw Pact forces in Eastern Europe and to adopt a more defensive posture, this could transform the security situation in Europe. This more than anything else would convince sceptics that a real change has taken place in Soviet security policy.

Gorbachev's pronouncements have been met with a good deal of scepticism in the West, and his concessions have been viewed by many as an attempt to undermine the policy of NATO. At best, the sceptics argue, Gorbachev is seeking a breathing space in international relations while he sets the Soviet economy to rights; at worst, he is trying to lure the West into abandoning key elements of its defence policy. It is difficult now to offer a definitive judgment on the 'new thinking'. It is no doubt designed to help the Soviet Union deal with its domestic problems; but it also appears to represent an attempt to move away from an autarchic, unilateral definition of security, in terms of military and industrial power, to a concept of security that rests on cooperative relations with other states in an interdependent world.

THE FUTURE

The answers the Soviet Union has given to the questions raised in the introduction to this chapter have changed, partly because the strategic nuclear relationship with the United States has moved from inferiority to parity. But the Soviet Union has also learned from the failures of Khrushchev's missile diplomacy and Brezhnev's detente

199

policy. Gorbachev is much more sceptical about the political and military utility of nuclear weapons than were his predecessors and has urged the world to opt for a non-nuclear future.

14

The Soviet Union in
Perspective

R. W. DAVIES

In the first few years after Gorbachev was appointed General Secretary of the Party in March 1985, little had changed on the surface of Soviet life. Queues continued in the shops; sometimes they were even longer than before. The quality of goods, and of food in restaurants and canteens, remained as poor as ever. The pace of work in factories and offices continued to be slower than in Britain, let alone in the United States or Japan.

But beneath the surface profound changes were at work. In my own view, by the end of 1987 *glasnost'* (openness) in the press and on television had already launched a mental revolution in the Soviet Union, which it would be very difficult to bring permanently to a halt. As I see it, the vast range of factual information, comment and opinion appearing in the Soviet media from the end of 1986 represented a huge shift to frankness of a kind that had not been seen since the 1920s, if then. This view is implicitly challenged in our pages. In Chapter 11, Professor G. S. Smith argues that the greater liveliness in literature and the arts did not, by the time of writing (the end of 1987), indicate a fundamental change in Party control.

Glasnost' is, however, only the beginning of the reconstruction (*perestroika*) of the economic, political and social structure and of everyday life. The plans and possibilities for revolutionary changes in Soviet society are a central theme of most chapters in this book. In Brezhnev's twilight years, very few Soviet citizens, and hardly any Western experts on the Soviet Union, even remotely anticipated such sweeping changes. But within two or three years of March 1985, most Western experts, and many Soviet citizens, were convinced that Gorbachev and his close associates *intended* to bring

201

about fundamental reforms, though there was a prevailing atmosphere of scepticism about their chances of success.

The most elaborate provisions for major changes, which had been approved by the beginning of 1988, concerned the economy. The desirability of economic reform was obvious even by the mid-1950s, and in the 30 years after Stalin's death several major but unsuccessful attempts were made to change the economic system (see Chs 3 and 7). From at least the mid-1960s, the Soviet Union failed to shorten its technological lag behind the advanced capitalist countries. By the mid-1970s, economic reform was an urgent necessity; the rate of economic growth had fallen so much that, for the first time since the Second World War, national output (the Gross National Product or GNP) was expanding less rapidly than in the United States and much more slowly than in newly-industrialised countries such as Japan. In Chapter 7, Professor Hanson argues that the planned reforms amount to a very substantial move towards 'market socialism'. Independent cooperatives and small-scale individual enterprises exist side-by-side with state ownership; for the state enterprises, detailed central planning from above is giving way to the influence of the consumer through the market. Philip Hanson is not at all sure that these measures will be realised in practice. Even if they are, he believes that improvements in economic performance will be modest. Without the fear of bankruptcy and the whip of unemployment, state enterprises will not be as innovative, and their workers will not be as productive, as in the capitalist world.

Dr Cooper's assessment of the economic reforms (Chapter 8) differs from that of Professor Hanson. He does not believe that they amount to a far-reaching move toward 'market socialism', but rather that they are important modifications to the existing system. Nevertheless, he expects that they will be effective enough, coupled with political reform, to enable the USSR to 'remain in the league of the major industrial nations'. It may be added that the debate about whether job insecurity is essential for economic progress rages throughout the capitalist world; in the hope of refuting Professor Hanson, some of us look back nostalgically to the 1950s and 1960s, when full employment was combined with rapid development in the capitalist as well as the socialist world.

Many Western experts on the Soviet Union believed that Gorbachev and his colleagues would confine their reforms to technical improvements in the economic system. On the contrary, since 1985 the Soviet leaders have insisted that radical economic reform must be accompanied or even preceded by profound changes in Soviet politics. Two different but complementary explanations of the present political reforms are found in this volume. In Chapter 4, Professor Lewin emphasises that in the post-war decades Soviet society has been transformed into a much more complex and diversified organism. It has become an urban society; two-thirds of the population now live in towns, as compared with one-third on the eve of the Second World War. In 1986, there were 15 million graduates in the USSR, as compared with 900000 on the eve of the Second World War and a mere 230000 in 1928. Even in the Brezhnev years, Moshe Lewin believed that these social changes would lead to major changes in the Soviet system; in the present volume, he concludes that corresponding reforms in the Party 'cannot be blocked for too long, nor can they be reversed'.

In Chapter 5, the second chapter on Soviet politics, Professor Amann explains the reforms by means of a close examination of the twists and turns of Soviet policy since the death of Stalin. He concludes that the radical economic decentralisation essential to the modernisation of the Soviet Union can be achieved only by overcoming the vested interests in the state and Party administration. These vested interests, which were created over a long period by the hierarchical system of central planning, have proved too powerful to be gently manipulated. Brezhnev's attempt to maintain political stability by balancing the key interests in the state — the arrangement that Ronald Amann calls 'state corporatism' — resulted in economic stagnation. Gorbachev seeks to overcome bureaucratic resistance to reform by increased democratisation, by popular participation in administration at the workplace and in government, and by the frank public discussion of problems and their solutions, which he regards as a precondition for economic reform.

The immense effort by Gorbachev and his supporters to achieve fundamental political reform was consolidated and intensified at the XIX Communist Party Conference in June 1988. Discussion was franker than at any time since 1927. The conference launched a programme which aims to increase the authority of the Soviets, extend democracy in the Party and the state, and strengthen the rule of law. Whether this programme is far-reaching enough to overcome the inertia of the past is hotly debated, both among Western commentators and among Soviet citizens.

To what extent will the drive for economic and political reform affect the nature of Soviet society? In Chapter 6, Professor Lane shows that, like other industrialised countries, the Soviet Union is a 'stratified' society, in which there is considerable inequality in income, status, and educational opportunity between and within the different social groups. These inequalities are partly a consequence of the division of labour between different types of occupations in a society that is still not very wealthy. The more interesting and influential jobs are much sought after, have high status, and accordingly carry high rewards. According to David Lane, the major inequalities are unlikely to be overcome until Soviet society is materially much wealthier. They are also sustained from generation to generation by the family and, in consequence, are likely to continue as long as family ties remain strong.

But there is another important reason for the persistence of social inequality in the USSR. As Lane points out, inequality is greatly strengthened by the varying political influence of different social groups. Greater popular participation at the place of work, and in political life generally, is likely to reduce the differences between those who give the orders and those who carry them out. But the crucial social problems of the USSR may have a more profound basis than this. Some Marxist critics of the Soviet system argue that Soviet society is dominated by a new kind of ruling class — what the Russians call the 'bossdom' (*nachal'stvo*). If this view is right, it is also certain that the thrust of *perestroika* has not so far been directed toward the destruction of the *nachal'stvo* as the dominant social group, but rather toward bringing it into a more flexible relationship with the other classes. In Marxist terms, or rather in terms used by the Trotskyist wing of Marxism, Gorbachev's democratisation aims to eliminate bureaucratic behaviour (*bureaucratism*), but not *the bureaucracy* as a dominant social class. Soviet economic and political reformers, including the top Party leadership, strongly emphasise that reform will carry with it greater rewards for harder and more efficient work; in the late 1980s, they reject equality of incomes as incompatible with socialism no less firmly than Stalin did when he attacked petty-bourgeois egalitarianism in 1931. But some of Gorbachev's more radical supporters regard the bureaucracy as a social class, as a creation of Stalinism, and as alien to socialism.

The urgent desire to reconstruct Soviet society has led Soviet intellectuals, followed somewhat reluctantly by the political leadership, to re-examine both the history of the Soviet period and the Russian pre-revolutionary past. If the Soviet Union in the 1970s was in a state of 'stagnation', as Gorbachev claimed, was this the result of taking the wrong road at earlier crossroads of history?

The question of alternatives or choices in Soviet history has preoccupied Western historians. The debates closely resemble older disputes about the English Civil War of the 1640s and the Glorious Revolution of 1688, and the French Revolution and the Napoleonic era. Two major moments of choice are discussed in our historical chapters: the Revolutions that overthrew Tsarism in 1917 and the triumph of Stalinism at the end of the 1920s. In Chapter 2, Mrs Perrie draws our attention to the influential view of some Western historians that, in the last decades before the First World War, Tsarist Russia was progressing toward a kind of capitalist constitutional monarchy. In this view it was the war, which they regard as a kind of accident, that disrupted this progress. Other historians emphasise the profound and irreconcilable social and political divisions within the Russian Empire in 1913, and also argue that the First World War was by no means an accidental event in Russian history, but a consequence of fundamental faults in the capitalist world order, of which Russia was a part. Maureen Perrie herself argues that whereas revolution against the Tsarist regime may have been inevitable in 1917, the launching of the October Revolution by Lenin and the Bolsheviks was a matter of human choice. The October Revolution was at first supported by the industrial working class, but this was a small minority of the whole population; in the turmoil that followed, Communist power was actively upheld only by a minority of this minority, together with a small number of intellectuals and peasants. Was the Russian Empire ready for socialism in 1917? Maureen Perrie suggests that this question can be answered by weighing the successes of the Bolshevik Revolution against its failures. On the one hand, there were major improvements in the standard of living and the quality of people's lives; on the other hand, there was repression, suffering and deprivation on a huge scale during the Stalin period.

Other difficult problems are involved in the evaluation of the Bolshevik Revolution. Soviet historians firmly insist, and they are supported here by many of their Western colleagues, that the alternative to the Bolshevik dictatorship was not some kind of parliamentary democracy, democratic capitalism, or peasant socialism, but a ruthless right-wing military dictatorship of the kind that flourished in the territories occupied by the anti-Bolshevik forces during the Civil War. In this view, the only choice was between a dictatorship of the Left and a dictatorship of the Right.

Another influential group of Western historians, supported by many Soviet intellectuals, strongly argues that the October Revolution cannot be fairly judged in terms of the experience of the Stalin dictatorship. In 1928–29, there was a second major moment of choice, when the relatively democratic mixed economy of the New Economic Policy (NEP) was replaced by what Mr Gorbachev has called 'the administrative–command system of party–state management of the country'. Perhaps a modified form of the New Economic Policy, which was a kind of social contract between the state, the peasants and the workers, could have provided a more humane means for transforming the Soviet Union into a great modern power?

Both the suffering and the achievements of the Stalin period were immense. The historical chapters in this volume draw attention to the human and economic losses and failures: the clumsiness of the economic system, the inhumanity of the expulsion of the *kulak* peasants from their lands and their villages, the viciousness of the successive purges (see Ch. 4), the blindness of Stalin to the threat of Nazi invasion in 1941, and the ineptness of Soviet post-war foreign policy (see Ch. 12).

But at the same time, as is argued in Chapter 3, Stalinist industrialisation transformed a largely peasant country into a modern industrial power and provided the economic basis for the victory over the Nazi invasion, by which the Soviet Union, together with its Western allies, saved world civilisation. The forced industrialisation of the 1930s was also the essential background to the post-war rise of the USSR into a super-power. And it had some positive social consequences: it was accompanied by the educational revolution described by Dr Dunstan in Chapter 10. The wider role of Soviet industrialisation in world economic history was to speed up greatly the transfer of modernisation from Europe and the United States into the Third World.

In Chapter 3, I take a favourable and perhaps old-fashioned view of industrialisation as such, but other chapters in this volume show that it was not an unmixed blessing. These alternative assessments are a particular version of the discussion about the value of rapid

206

economic growth, which is taking place throughout the world in the closing years of this century. In Chapter 9, Professor R. E. F. Smith expresses strong doubts about whether Soviet industrialisation was worthwhile from the point of view of the mass of the population, in view of the disasters in agriculture that accompanied it. Until recent decades, the immense gulf between town and country, the great social weakness of 19th-century Russia, continued to be as wide as ever: it still remains wide today. And in Chapter 1, Dr Shaw, while comparing the achievements of past and present Soviet industrialisers in overcoming the immense difficulties imposed by an inhospitable climate, also draws our attention to the extensive pollution of air and water that were the consequences of industrialisation in Russia, at least as much as in other countries. In a later phase of Soviet industrialisation, industrial carelessness with land, water, and other natural resources (typical of socialist as well as capitalist industrialisers) led to the world's worst nuclear accident at Chernobyl in the Ukraine in April 1986.

An eternally fascinating question is raised particularly forcefully by Russian and Soviet experience: the role of the individual in history and politics. There is no doubt that the Tsars and their successors, the General Secretaries of the Communist Party, have wielded immense power. But how decisive was this power in determining the major changes in society? The implicit answers in this book vary from author to author and period to period. Maureen Perrie puts the case for the role of the individual quite strongly in Chapter 2; she argues that the attitude of Tsar Nicholas II was a major obstacle to the extension of democracy in pre-revolutionary Russia, and that Lenin was personally responsible for the decision to launch the October Revolution of 1917 and impose a one-party dictatorship. In my own account of Soviet industrialisation in Chapter 3, Stalin is, not surprisingly, very prominent, though I would argue that Stalin's personality modified rather than fundamentally determined the course of Soviet history in the 1930s. When we come to Gorbachev, the role of his personal initiative in pressing ahead with *glasnost'* and *perestroika* is obvious. But at the same time, our chapters on the economy, society, and politics have all shown that conditions had long been ripe for a major change. Perhaps historians in future generations will ask not how Gorbachev came to embark on radical reform but why his predecessors were so timorous.

However powerful the Soviet leader, he and his country are constrained by a dangerous and complex world. Over many centuries, Russia has had to face the crucial problem, first as a great European power and then as a great world power, that she was economically weaker than her major rivals. From 1917 to 1945, Soviet Russia was the only country in which a Communist-led revolution had succeeded; the Soviet state faced an unfriendly world alone (see Ch. 12). In 1918–19, it had to cope with the military intervention of much stronger powers. In the 1920s, the defeat of revolution in Germany and China, followed by the war scares of 1926–27, played an important part in the decision to industrialise at breakneck speed. In the 1930s, the victory of the Nazis, with their policies of destroying Communism and conquering and subjugating the whole of Europe, meant that the Soviet Union had to develop defence industries strong enough to compete with those of the economically advanced Nazi Germany. This made the struggle to industrialise both much more urgent and more difficult.

In its international relations in the 40 years following the end of the Second World War, the Soviet Union was concerned with avoiding war while taking advantage of revolutionary upheaval to extend its power. But such actions as the invasion of South Korea in 1950 greatly strengthened the position of those people in the United States and Western Europe who believed that a 'Russian threat' was hanging over the world and must be met with massive rearmament. Throughout the 1950s and 1960s, the Soviet Union was militarily and diplomatically weaker than the United States, whose enormous economic and political power dominated the globe. In the 1970s, with the United States weakened by the disastrous Vietnam war, Brezhnev sought to end Soviet military weakness, and achieved nuclear parity; simultaneously, the Soviet Union and its allies gave military and political support to revolutionary movements in Africa and elsewhere. The West reacted sharply. By the early 1980s, a new arms race and a 'new Cold War' were well under way. Historians are deeply divided about how the blame for the tense relations that have prevailed since the Second World War should be apportioned between the Soviet Union and the Western powers.

What is certain is that the continued arms race has had disastrous consequences for the Soviet economy. Today, with a GNP only one-half that of the United States, the USSR still has to devote twice as high a proportion of it to defence as does the United States (see

Ch. 7) if it is not to fall behind its adversary. This has greatly exacerbated all the difficulties of the ageing Soviet economic structure, which is faced with an outside world experiencing a new technological revolution.

Since 1985, Soviet foreign and strategic policies have been drastically modified. A series of Soviet initiatives in diplomacy and major concessions in arms control resulted in the agreement to remove Intermediate Nuclear Forces from Europe, reached by Reagan and Gorbachev at the December 1985 summit. International arms control will undoubtedly make it much easier for the Soviet Union to find resources for economic progress.

In Chapters 12 and 13, Professors Haslam and Holloway show that Soviet international 'new thinking' is inspired by much broader considerations than the undoubtedly urgent economic need to reduce the defence burden. The two authors emphasise different aspects of Gorbachev's foreign policy. Jonathan Haslam argues that, in one aspect, it is 'purely tactical' — a new form of the Soviet ideological challenge to the West. David Holloway shows us how, in the course of tortuous debates over 35 years, the view that a nuclear holocaust would destroy civilisation became the central feature of Soviet foreign policy. He concludes that the new policy embodies a genuine new vision of international security, a move to a security system based on 'cooperative relations with other states in an interdependent world'. Haslam also agrees that Soviet foreign policy since 1985 is a 'bold attempt to remove . . . rivalry from the military to the political arena'.

Another close connection between internal reform and external policy has been strongly emphasised by Gorbachev. He hopes that successful economic reform would enable the Soviet Union to become an integral and influential part of the world economic system, which in turn would greatly strengthen the emerging world system of peace and international security. It might be added that a long-term success for *glasnost'* and *perestroika*, bringing the humanisation of the Soviet system together with substantial economic and technological progress, would do much on a world scale to advance the prestige of socialism by the end of the 20th century. But such speculation about a golden Soviet future — alluring for some of us, unattractive for others — may perhaps exceed the rights of an editor.

Appendix
Soviet History:
Some Major Events

1861		Liberation of the serfs
1890s		First industrialisation drive
1894		Nicholas II succeeds to Imperial throne
1905		First Russian Revolution
1914		Outbreak of Great War (First World War)
1916	December	Murder of Rasputin
1917	February–March	Revolution overthrows Tsar, establishes 'Dual Power'
	October–November	Revolution establishes Bolshevik or Soviet Government
1918	January	Constituent Assembly dissolved
	March	Treaty of Brest-Litovsk signed by Soviet Russia with Germany
1918–20		Civil War and foreign intervention
1919	March	Communist International founded
1921–29		New Economic Policy (NEP)
1921	March	X Congress of Communist Party ends requisitioning of grain and bans 'groupings' within Party
1922		Rapallo Treaty signed by Soviet Russia with Germany
1923		Constitution of Union of Soviet Socialist Republics approved
1924	January	Death of Lenin
1926–7		Chinese Communists defeated by Chiang Kai-shek
1926–28		Pre-First World War output of industry and agriculture restored
October 1928–December 1932		First five-year plan
End 1929		Drive to collectivise agriculture launched
1931		Japanese invasion of Manchuria
1933		Hitler comes to power in Germany

1933–37		Second five-year plan
1934		USSR joins League of Nations and supports Collective Security
1936	August	Outbreak of Spanish Civil War
1936–38		'Great Purges'
1936	December	'Stalin Constitution' adopted
1941	22 June	German invasion of USSR
1941	October	Moscow under siege
1942	November	Soviet victory at Stalingrad
1943	July	Soviet victory in Kursk tank battle
1945	9 May	Victory over Germany
1947–54		'Cold War'
1949		Pre-Second World War output of industry and agriculture restored, Chinese Communists victorious in Civil War
1953	March	Death of Stalin
1955–present		'Peaceful coexistence' with West
1956	February	Khrushchev denounces Stalin at XX Party Congress
1957–65		Regional economic councils established
1960		Soviet economic and technical aid to China cancelled
1962	October	Cuban missile crisis
1964	October	Khrushchev replaced by Brezhnev and Kosygin
1965		'Kosygin' economic reform
1968		'Prague Spring', Soviet invasion of Czechoslovakia (August)
1972		SALT I (Strategic Arms Limitations Treaty), Anti-Ballistic Missile Treaty signed
1979		SALT II, not ratified by United States
1979	December	Soviet invasion of Afghanistan
1982	November	Death of Brezhnev, replaced by Andropov
1984	February	Death of Andropov, replaced by Chernenko
1985	March	Gorbachev succeeds Chernenko
1987	January	Central Committee plenum widens scope of reform
	June	Economic reforms approved
	December	INF (Intermediate-Range Nuclear Forces) Treaty agreed to at Reagan–Gorbachev meeting in Washington
1988	June	XIX Conference of Communist Party

Glossary and Abbreviations

ABM	Anti-Ballistic Missile
ASSR	Autonomous Soviet Socialist Republic (subordinate to Union Republic)
Bolsheviks	More revolutionary section, headed by Lenin, of Russian Social Democratic Labour Party (so called from the Russian *bol'shinstvo* — majority, because they obtained a majority of the votes at one stage in the 1903 Congress)
Bourgeoisie (capitalist class)	In Marxist theory, the class that owns the means of production and exploits the proletariat under capitalism
Brezhnev, L. I.	(1906–82) General (formerly First) Secretary of the Communist Party of the Soviet Union (the leading political figure), 1964–82
Bukharin, N. I.	(1888–1938) Bolshevik leader, prominent intellectual in 1920s, headed Right opposition 1928–29, executed 1938, rehabilitated 1988
Communism	In Marxist theory, in the higher stage of Communism when goods are abundant, means of production will be publicly owned as under socialism, but distribution will be according to the principle 'from each according to ability, to each according to need', not according to work done, and the distinction between mental and manual labour and town and country will be abolished
Constituent Assembly	Parliament established in 1917 with universal equal franchise, dissolved by the Bolsheviks in January 1918
Duma	Pre-Revolutionary parliament with limited powers and franchise, established 1906

212

Glasnost'	Openness (frankness in public discussion), one of the slogans of the post-March 1985 reform programme
Glavk (*glavnoe upravlenie*)	Chief Administration, major sub-division of a Soviet ministry (plural glavki)
Glavlit (*glavnoe literaturnoe upravlenie*)	Chief Literary Administration, the Soviet censorship office
Gorbachev, M. S.	(b. 1931) General Secretary of the Communist Party of the Soviet Union, 1985–
GNP	Gross National Product
Gosplan (*Gosudarstvennaya planovaya komissiya*, later *Gosudarstvennyi planovyi komitet*)	State Planning Commission (Committee)
ICBM	Inter-Continental Ballistic Missile
INF	Intermediate-Range Nuclear Forces
Intelligentsia	In Soviet terminology, refers to the white-collar workers or 'workers by brain', not engaged directly in production (usually refers only to those in this group with some professional or semi-professional skill)
KGB (*Komitet gosudarstvennoi beszopasnosti*)	Committee of State Security (responsible for political police)
Khrushchev, N. S.	(1894–1971) First Secretary of the Communist Party of the Soviet Union (the leading political figure) 1953–64, Chairman of Council of Ministers of USSR (equal to Prime Minister) 1957–64
Kosygin, A. I.	(1904–80) Chairman of Council of Ministers of USSR (equal to Prime Minister) 1964–80
Lenin, V. I.	(1871–1924) Leader of Bolsheviks before and after October Revolution
Litvinov, M. M.	(1876–1951) People's Commissar for Foreign Affairs 1930–9
Marx, Karl	(1818–83) Founder of scientific Communism
Marxism-Leninism	Soviet term for the official ideology of the Communist party, from its founders Marx and Lenin
Mensheviks	Less revolutionary section of Russian Social Democratic Labour Party (from

213

	men'shinstvo — minority), see Bolsheviks
Molotov, V. M.	(1890–1986) Old Bolshevik, Chairman of Council of Ministers of USSR (equal to Prime Minister) 1930–41, People's Commissar (later Minister) of Foreign Affairs 1939–57
NATO	North Atlantic Treaty Organisation
Narkomindel (*Narodnyi komissariat inostrannykh del*)	People's Commissariat (equal to Ministry) of Foreign Affairs
NEP	New Economic Policy (Soviet policy introduced in 1921 permitting peasants freedom of trade on market, while continuing state ownership of large-scale industry)
NKVD (*Narodnyi komissariat vnutrennikh del*)	People's Commissariat (equal to Ministry) of Internal Affairs (formerly responsible for political police)
Oblast'	Region (unit of local government within one of the fifteen Union Republics — q.v.)
Perestroika	Reconstruction (revolutionary remoulding of society), one of the slogans of the post-March 1985 reform programme
Peter the Great (Peter I)	Tsar of Russia 1682–1725, reformed and westernised Russia by brutal means and hence often seen as precursor of Stalin
Politburo	Political Bureau of Central Committee of Communist Party of the Soviet Union, responsible for major policy decisions
Proletariat (working class)	In Marxist theory, the wage-earning class under capitalism, sells its labour power to the bourgeoisie and is exploited by them
R and D	Research and Development (see Ch. 8)
Rasputin, G.	'Holy man' from Siberia who preached redemption through sin, strongly influential on Empress and Court 1905–16
Samizdat	'Self-publishing', officially unacceptable writings, privately copied and disseminated in USSR
SLBM	Submarine-Launched Ballistic Missile
Socialism	In Marxist theory, the first or lower stage of Communism; factories, mines, and other means of production are publicly owned, distribution is on the principle

	'from each according to ability, to each according to work done'
Soviet	Russian word for council, originally the name of local revolutionary organs elected by workers, soldiers, and peasants, now the name of local and central government organs in USSR
SPTU (*srednee professional'no-tekhnicheskoe uchilishche*)	Secondary vocational and technical school
SRs	Socialist Revolutionaries (pre-Revolutionary, pro-peasant party)
Stalin, I. V.	(1879–1953) General Secretary of Communist Party 1922–53, dominant political leader from about 1928 to 1953
Stolypin, P. A.	(1862–1911) Russian statesman, Chairman of Council of Ministers 1906–11, suppressed revolution and carried out agrarian reforms, assassinated by SR terrorist who was also police agent
Tons	Metric tons (tonnes) are used throughout this volume
Trotsky, L. D.	(1879–1940) Soviet revolutionary leader, People's Commissar for War 1918–25, headed Left opposition in 1920s, expelled from USSR 1929, murdered 1940
Tsar	Monarch (emperor) in pre-Revolutionary Russian Empire
Union Republic	One of the fifteen republics that make up the USSR
USSR	Union of Soviet Socialist Republics, also known as the Soviet Union and (inaccurately) as Soviet Russia (the Russians similarly refer to Great Britain as England)
Vuz (plural vuzy) (*Vysshee uchebnoe zavedenie*)	Higher educational establishment(s), including both universities and higher technical educational establishments (vtuzy)

Bibliography

CHAPTER I: THE GEOGRAPHICAL REALITY

Cole, J. P. *Geography of the Soviet Union* (London: Butterworths, 1984).
Lydolph, P. E. *Geography of the USSR*, 3rd edn (New York: John Wiley, 1977).
Lydolph, P. E. *Geography of the USSR: Topical Analysis* (Elkhart Lake, Wisconsin: Misty Valley, 1979).
Parker, W. H. *'The World's Landscapes'. 3. The Soviet Union* (London: Longman, 1969).
Pryde, P. R. *Conservation in the Soviet Union* (Cambridge: Cambridge University Press, 1972).
Symons, L. (ed.) *The Soviet Union: A Systematic Geography* (London: Hodder and Stoughton, 1983).
Wood, A. (ed.) *Siberia: Problems and Prospects for Regional Development* (London: Croom Helm, 1987).

CHAPTER 2: THE OCTOBER REVOLUTION

Chamberlin, W. H. *The Russian Revolution, 1917–1921*, 2 Vols (London: Macmillan, 1935).
Kochan, L. *Russia in Revolution, 1890–1918* (London: Paladin, 1970).
Mawdsley, E. *The Russian Civil War* (London: Allen & Unwin, 1987).
Rabinowitch, A. *The Bolsheviks Come to Power* (New York: Norton, 1976).
Rogger, H. *Russia in the Age of Modernisation and Revolution, 1881–1917* (London: Longman, 1983).

CHAPTER 3: INDUSTRIALISATION AND AFTER

Carr, E. H. *The Russian Revolution from Lenin to Stalin* (London: Macmillan, 1978).
Fitzpatrick, S. *The Russian Revolution* (Oxford: OUP, 1982).
Lewin, M. *The Making of the Soviet System* (London: Methuen, 1985).
Nove, A. *An Economic History of the USSR* (Harmondsworth: Pelican, revised 1982).
Von Laue, T. H. *Why Lenin? Why Stalin?* (London: Weidenfeld & Nicolson, 1966).

216

CHAPTER 4: THE COMMUNIST PARTY, YESTERDAY AND TODAY

Deutscher, I. *The Unfinished Revolution, 1917–1967* (London: Oxford University Press, 1967).

Lane, D. S. *State and Politics in the USSR* (London: Blackwell, 1985).

Lenin, V. I. *What Is to Be Done?* (first published in 1902); *State and Revolution* (first published 1917); these pamphlets are included in several editions of Lenin's writings.

CHAPTER 5: SOVIET POLITICS: PERSPECTIVES AND PROSPECTS

Bialer, S. *Stalin's Successors: Leadership, Stability and Change in the Soviet Union* (Cambridge: Cambridge University Press, 1988).

Gorbachev, M. *Perestroika: New Thinking for Our Country and the World* (London, Collins, 1987).

Hill, R. J. and P. Frank (eds) *The Soviet Communist Party*, 3rd edn (London: Allen & Unwin, 1986).

McCauley, M. (ed.) *The Soviet Union under Gorbachev* (London: Macmillan, 1987).

CHAPTER 6: SOCIAL CLASSES AND EQUALITY

Djilas, M. *The New Class* (London: George Allen & Unwin, 1957).

Lane, D. S. *The End of Inequality?* (Harmondsworth: Penguin, 1971).

Parkin, F. *Class, Inequality and Political Order* (London: Paladin, 1970).

CHAPTER 7: THE ECONOMIC SYSTEM

Gregory, P. R. and R. C. Stuart *Soviet Economic Structure and Performance*, 2nd edn (New York: Harper and Row, 1981).

Nove, A. *The Soviet Economic System* (London: Allen & Unwin, 1977).

US Congress Joint Economic Committee, *Gorbachev's Economic Plans* (Washington, DC: U.S. Government Printing Office, 2 vols, 1987). A collection of papers by leading Western specialists: detailed, but up-to-date and wide ranging.

CHAPTER 8: SCIENCE AND TECHNOLOGY

Amann, R. and J. M. Cooper (eds) *Technical Progress and Soviet Economic Development* (Oxford: Basil Blackwell, 1986).

Berry, M. J. (ed.) *Science and Technology in the USSR* (Harlow: Longman, 1988).

Fortescue, S. *The Communist Party and Soviet Science* (London: Macmillan, 1986).

217

Medvedev, Z. A. *Soviet Science* (Oxford: Oxford University Press, 1979).

CHAPTER 9: FARMS AND FARMERS

Lewin, M. *Russian Peasants and Soviet Power* (London: George Allen & Unwin, 1968).
Medvedev, Z. A. *Soviet Agriculture* (NY–London: Norton, 1987).
Robinson, G. T. *Rural Russia under the Old Regime* (Berkeley: University of California Press, 1967).
Strauss, E. *Soviet Agriculture in Perspective* (London: George Allen & Unwin, 1969).
Symons, L. *Russian Agriculture: A Geographic Survey* (London: Bell, 1972).

CHAPTER 10: THE EDUCATION OF THE SOVIET CITIZEN

Avis, G. (ed.) *The Making of the Soviet Citizen* (London: Croom Helm, 1987).
Bronfenbrenner, U. *Two Worlds of Childhood* (Harmondsworth: Penguin, 1974).
Grant, N. *Soviet Education*, 4th edn (Harmondsworth: Penguin, 1979).
Matthews, M. *Education in the Soviet Union* (London: George Allen & Unwin, 1982).
Muckle, J. *A Guide to the Soviet Curriculum* (London: Croom Helm, 1988).

CHAPTER 11: LITERATURE AND THE ARTS

Brown, E. J. *Russian Literature since the Revolution* (London: Harvard University Press, revised 1982).
Hingley, R. *Russian Writers and Soviet Society, 1917–1978* (London: Weidenfeld and Nicholson, 1979).
Labedz, L. (ed.) *Solzhenitsyn: A Documentary Record* (Harmondsworth: Penguin, 1972).
Proffer, C. 'Russian Writing and Border Guards — Twenty-Five Years of the New Isolationism', in his *The Widows of Russia and Other Writings* (Ann Arbor: University of Michigan Press, 1987).
Smith, G. S. *Songs to Seven Strings: Russian Guitar Poetry and Soviet 'Mass Song'* (Bloomington: University of Indiana Press, 1984).

CHAPTER 12: FOREIGN POLICY

Beloff, M. *The Foreign Policy of Soviet Russia, 1929–1941*, Vols 1–3 (London: Oxford University Press, 1968).
Fischer, L. *The Soviets in World Affairs*, Vols 1–2 (London: Jonathan Cape, 1930).

Haslam, J. *Soviet Foreign Policy, 1930–33: the Impact of the Depression* (London: Macmillan, 1983).

Haslam, J. *The Soviet Union and the Struggle for Collective Security in Europe, 1933–39* (London: Macmillan, 1984).

Steele, J. *World Powers: Soviet Foreign Policy under Brezhnev and Andropov* (London: Joseph, 1982).

CHAPTER 13: THE SOVIET FUTURE IN A NUCLEAR AGE

Gorbachev, M. *Perestroika: New Thinking for Our Country and the World* (London: Collins, 1987).

Holloway, D. *The Soviet Union and the Arms Race* (New Haven and London: Yale University Press, 1983).

Pryns, G. *Defended to Death: A Study of the Nuclear Arms Race* (London: Penguin, 1983).

Shenfield, S. *The Nuclear Predicament: Explorations in Soviet Ideology* (London: Routledge, 1987).

Talbott, S. *Deadly Gambits: The Reagan Administration and the Stalemate in Arms Control* (London: Picador, 1984).

Index

227

For Product Safety Concerns and Information please contact our EU
representative GPSR@taylorandfrancis.com
Taylor & Francis Verlag GmbH, Kaufingerstraße 24, 80331 München, Germany

www.ingramcontent.com/pod-product-compliance
Lightning Source LLC
Chambersburg PA
CBHW050425280326
41932CB00013BA/2000

9 7 8 1 0 3 2 6 7 6 3 5 7